PRAIS

OFF THE PAGE & INTO YOUR LIFE

With an encouraging and compelling style, Tami Weissert weaves seven approaches to spending time with God and His Word into something everyone can tackle. With real-life stories and unique applications, she provides a personal, customizable game plan that feels like you are sitting with your favorite mentor. Her suggestions are a great way to dive into God's Word!

—Sherry Surratt, CEO and President, MOPS International

If you are like me, it can be a challenge to find words in the Bible relevant for your daily life. Tami Weissert has found a way. *Off the Page & Into Your Life* follows people as they learn to "experience" the Bible. If that sounds like you, then this book is a must read.

—Mike Novac, CEO and President, K-LOVE and Air1 Radio Networks

Tami has deepened my experience with the Bible in true, practical ways. Her roll-up-your-sleeves-and-get-started approach to using your life circumstances to grow and connect to God is spot on. I can't wait to dig in and give some of these ideas a try for myself. This is a book you will keep with your Bible and reference again and again.

—Diana Goldy, Director of Outreach and Sales, MOPS International

Finally, an easy-to-digest book on how the Bible integrates with real life! No heaping helping of guilt, just thought-provoking examples that help anyone uniquely plug in to the power of God's Word. Tami's stories and instruction spark the imagination and make interfacing with God's Word not just possible but an exciting part of regular day-to-day life. Practical, penetrating, positive; uncomplicated, compelling, and richly rewarding.

—Nancy Sebastian Meyer, Author of *Talk Easy, Listen Hard*

This is the most creative and compelling book I've read for not only giving options for how to engage God's Word, but for showing the benefits with real data! The women in these chapters teach how to make the Bible come alive through their own pain. Each found and implemented their personal method of discovering God's Word to be exciting, necessary, and alive. Reading this book will allow you to grow in your relationship with God, as you find yourself among the statistics in the appendix!

> **—Ruth M. Davis, President and COO,**
> **Pennsylvania Counseling Services**

I found great value in the practical way Weissert guides the reader in forming a deliberate and active response to each biblical lesson. Whether through journaling or the "Take it In, Live it Out" process, faith is both encouraged to stretch and to grow deeper. If you want to know God better, then get to know His Word. *Off the Page & Into Your Life* does exactly that!

> **—Lucinda Secrest McDowell, Author of *Live These Words***

When an individual learns to move from reading the Bible to engaging with it, the human condition is touched by the miraculous message of God. This book helps us see how the reality of our lives can be changed from a negative story to one that represents the power of God being displayed in everyday events. The stories of lives changed as a result of meeting Jesus serve as an important reminder that God is available to change us too.

> **—Roy Smith, PhD, Author and Founder,**
> **Knights of the 21st Century Ministry**

Lots of people talk about the importance of the Bible. Then there are those who actually read it, discovering powerful words capable of transforming you by changing the way you think. *Off The Page & Into Your Life* will move you into the exciting adventure of living in God's Word—you will no longer need to wonder how to glean the treasure found in the Bible.

> **—Catherine Martin, Author and Speaker,**
> **Founder of Quiet Time Ministries**

TAMI WEISSERT

OFF THE PAGE & INTO YOUR LIFE

GETTING MORE FROM GOD'S WORD
NO MATTER WHAT YOUR STORY

Authentic

Off the Page & Into Your Life

©2014 by Tami Weissert

Cover design by Peter Gloege | LOOK Design Studio
Edited by Jeff Braun

Published by Authentic Publishers
188 Front Street, Suite 116-44
Franklin, TN 37064

Authentic Publishers is a division of
Authentic Media, Inc.

Library of Congress Cataloging-in-Publication Data
Weissert, Tami
      Off the Page & Into Your Life: Getting more from god's word—no matter what your story / Tami Weissert
p. cm.

ISBN 978-1-78078-116-7
      978-1-78078-238-6 (eBook)

Printed in the United States of America
21 20 19 18 17 16 15 14   10 9 8 7 6 5 4 3 2 1

In memory of my dad and mom,
Darrell and Betty Smith.

Thank you for bringing me up in a
loving Christian home where God and the Bible
were front and center. Your personal examples of
daily being in the Word and living for Christ
continue to influence, motivate and inspire me.

Frie -

CONTENTS

ACKNOWLEDGMENTS

To the many people who helped with this book. I couldn't have done it without you:

Jeff Weissert, my precious husband. You are my best friend and biggest supporter. Thank you for talking through ideas for the book with me, and then reading every chapter through each round of revisions. You are truly a gem, and I appreciate you helping me stay focused and moving forward on this project.

Dr. Arnie Cole, CEO of Back to the Bible and director of research and development for the Center for Bible Engagement. Your passion for getting people engaged in God's Word and growing spiritually—both as a researcher and practically—has been, and continues to be, a huge encouragement and motivator to me. Thank you for your support and for pushing me to step out and write this book. I'm grateful for this opportunity to help others engage the Bible.

Michael Ross, author and speaker, director of Back to the Bible's book publishing efforts. Thank you for championing Bible engagement through book writing, and for encouraging me to move into that realm as well. Our many discussions and your helpful suggestions and words of direction have been invaluable.

Dr. Pamela Ovwigho, executive director of the Center for Bible Engagement (CBE). Thank you for your passion for researching Bible engagement (preparing, administering and analyzing over 130,000 surveys over the past eight years), and for the impact the CBE research has had in the creation and development of *goTandem* and the ongoing ministry of Back to the Bible.

Meredith Megrue. You have been a constant encourager for me. Thank you for your friendship, listening to ideas, helping me with wording, and most importantly, coming up with the name for this book! I am grateful for you.

Margot Starbuck. Thank you for walking with me to get this book project up and going, and for just the right words of encouragement and direction when I needed them.

Greg Johnson, president of WordServe Literary Group in Colorado. You guided me through every step of the book writing process. Thank you. You are an excellent agent!

Jeff Braun, editor. You were the perfect person to edit this book. Thank you for your careful attention to the presentation of each story and flow of the book. Your suggestions and insight were so helpful. It was a joy working with you.

Kyle Duncan and the Authentic team. Thank you for loving God's Word and encouraging others to open their Bibles and engage it with me.

"*Life is complicated,*

hard, and downright messy.

But when you have a relationship

with God and you're

spending time in His Word,

you can live fully and well—

having hope, joy, and peace,

in and through all

of your circumstances."

INTRODUCTION

The Adventure

IN THESE PAGES, I'm inviting you into an adventure that will change your life.

I'm Tami Weissert, and I work at a ministry called Back to the Bible. Back to the Bible has been around for over seventy-five years, and is well known for its Bible teaching and for helping people of all ages engage God's Word through radio, the Internet, and mobile technologies.

Let me tell you a little about what I do. I am the executive vice president and in-house counsel for Back to the Bible. I also head up the ministry's Bible Engagement Division, which I absolutely love because it gives me the opportunity to encourage people, especially women, to get up-close and personal with God's Word.

I speak to women's groups around the country, write for the ministry, and am the blogging voice of *Powered by 4,* an online Bible engagement ministry of Back to the Bible. I was also the co-host of the *Back to the Bible* radio program for over eight years. I am thankful for all of these unique roles, because through them I have experienced firsthand just how important engaging God's Word is for life.

BIBLE ENGAGER

Today, I'm a Bible engager. In other words, central to my life is receiving, reflecting on, and responding to God's Word. Why is this so important? Well, life is complicated, hard, and downright messy. But when you have a relationship with God and you're spending time in His Word, you can live fully and well—having hope, joy, and peace, in and through all of your circumstances.

THERE ISN'T A ONE-SIZE-FITS-ALL WAY TO ENGAGE GOD'S WORD.

Unfortunately, for many years, I didn't connect the dots regarding the importance of understanding God's Word and living it out in my life. This led to heartaches, disappointments, failures, and hurts. Yes, I was a Christian, but my focus wasn't on God or His Word. Instead, it was on me—what I wanted, what I felt, what I thought would satisfy me. I was confident that I knew what was best for me and that I was in control of my life. Maybe this sounds familiar?

GOD IS SPEAKING TO YOU!

God created us to be in relationship with Him, and He gave us His Word, the Bible, so we can hear His voice and get to know His heart and mind. This means the best way to grow closer to God is to spend time in His Word. It's there where we learn who God is, and it's where He reveals His love and care for us as our Creator.

But there isn't a one-size-fits-all way to engage God's Word and grow closer to Him. That's because God created each one of us uniquely. So being the distinct people we are, we will each connect with and learn from God's Word a little differently. So how you prefer to spend time in God's Word won't look exactly like how your best friend, your sister, or even your mom spends time in the Bible. It took me a while to realize this, and it's one of the reasons I'm so excited to share *Off the Page & Into Your Life* with you.

As you read this book, here's what you can expect: In each chapter you'll get to know a different woman and the ups and downs of her specific story. What you'll find is that each woman has her own unique way of connecting with God through His Word. That's key, because at the end of each chapter you and I are going to try each woman's approach for ourselves, so we can experience a number of different ways to spend time with God and interact with Him through His Word.

I'll take the lead. I've actually done each chapter's exercise and included my responses so you can see my experience—what I considered, how I processed, and what I wrote. Hopefully this will be an encouragement for you to jump in yourself. I'm suggesting you try each approach for at least one week, and perhaps even a little longer; you be the judge. This will allow you to really get familiar with the approach, and in so doing, experience it more fully.

By the time you finish *Off the Page & Into Your Life,* you will have experienced seven different approaches to spending time with God through His Word. It's my hope that one or more of these will be used by God to speak to your heart and draw you closer to Him and further into His life-changing Word.

WARNING

If you say "yes" to the adventure ahead, know that as you set your heart to hear from God, you can expect some opposition. Satan doesn't want you seeking God and growing in your relationship with Him. So you'd better believe that keeping you away from God—and especially God's Word—is a priority for the enemy.

Satan loves to plant ideas in our head about why we can't possibly read our Bible and why we can't possibly have a meaningful relationship with God. He is *the* absolute master at lying and manipulation.

I can't tell you how many times I've bought into the lies and half-truths Satan has planted in my mind about spending time in my Bible. Here are a few:

+ I didn't read my Bible last week and nothing bad happened, so maybe I don't really need to read it.

+ I'm such a sinner, so why bother reading the Bible? God could never really love me anyway.

+ If God really loved me, why did He let "x" happen?

+ I've been going to church and doing my best to read my Bible and things still aren't turning out the way I thought. So why bother?

+ I just don't have time to read the Bible, and besides, I'm doing all right.

+ I couldn't possibly understand the Bible because it's so complex and difficult.

The truth is, God is speaking to you and me through the Bible. So don't give Satan even one fraction of an inch to keep you away from it. God gave His Word to all of us, so let's take full advantage of this, taking it in and living it out in our daily lives!

Now maybe you're thinking, *I've tried this all before and I just can't do it.* That's Satan's hiss. None of us can go back and change what we did yesterday. So there's no benefit to beating yourself up for what's done and over. Believe me, I've been there and done it, and it didn't help me one bit.

Today is a new day, so no matter what amount of time you've been spending in God's Word—and that means from zero minutes to most of the day—your time in the Word and with God can be incredible this very day. That's the truth, and as you go forward it can always get better.

CHAPTER 1

MAKING SCRIPTURE PERSONAL:

MY STORY

"In short order I'd fixate on one of those 'what-ifs,' and then I'd proceed to obsess over it. The initial what-if would lead to another, worse what-if and then another and another. And as I moved down the what-if path, I would get more and more anxious, frantic, irrational. It was awful. And even worse, once the cycle began, I couldn't control it. In fact, the more I tried to take control, the worse I got."

I WAS EIGHT YEARS OLD when I made the most important decision of my life.

It was a night pretty much like most nights in the Smith household. I watched TV with my dad, mom, and brother, and when the news came on, it was time for me to go to bed. I put on my pjs, brushed my teeth, and hollered to my mom that I was ready.

On this particular night, before my mom and I prayed, I told her I wanted to go to heaven. I don't recall why heaven was on my mind, but it was. So we knelt at the side of my bed and I prayed and asked Jesus into my heart. It is the best decision I've ever made, and it changed my life forever.

My dad and mom loved God and they loved His Word. Their Bibles, Dad's black and my Mom's bright red with gold edging on the pages, were on the end tables in our living room. Both were worn from use. I didn't fully appreciate what godly examples my parents were at the time, but looking back, I couldn't have had a better home environment to grow up in.

My family lived in a rural farming community of about six thousand people. We attended a small, conservative Bible-teaching church. Everybody knew everybody. Church felt like a big family gathering, and I loved it. I was in church Sunday morning, Sunday night, Wednesday night, and when I got old enough, Monday night for Awana, the Bible-based youth program. I was, quite literally, *raised* in church.

Overall, life growing up was pretty good. Contrary to the rebellious teen stereotype, I had a strong relationship with both my parents. I enjoyed school, got good grades, and didn't hang out with the partying crowd. If you had asked me about Jesus, my response would have been to tell you I believed in, and loved, the Lord. Even so, one thing was missing—personal time with God in His Word—and that proved to be detrimental to me.

A CHANGE OF DIRECTION

Once I headed to college, things changed fairly quickly. There I was, three hours from home—in the "big city"— and, wow, was it exciting. In my eyes, it was an adventure. And the biggest attraction? You guessed it—cute guys. Every weekend and most weeknights there were numerous opportunities to socialize, meet guys, and have fun. Basically, I moved away from home, met the world, and fell in love with it. The world grabbed me. It wasn't an intentional, planned thing. I wasn't being defiant toward my parents or anything like that. I just wanted to have fun. So without consulting God or my parents, I decided, just like that, to live for Tami. Almost immediately I stopped going to church and my focus turned to having a good time. Needless to say, I definitely wasn't living for the Lord, and I certainly wasn't concerned about reading my Bible.

About a year into college, I met Jeff. He was a Christian (not that I was looking for one) and a super nice guy. But like me, he wasn't going to church and wasn't seeking God through His Word. We got married and almost immediately our focus was on having material things and being successful in the world's eyes. This became what drove us.

Jeff, being an excellent student, graduated with honors with a degree in physical therapy from the University of Nebraska Medical Center. Soon after, I finished my undergraduate degree, and then went on to law school. During the entire eight- to ten-year period, Jeff and I were following our plan. We were in control, or so we thought. Of course, we weren't, but we sure operated that way.

> MY ATTITUDE WAS "I LOVE YOU, LORD, AND IF I NEED YOU, I'LL CALL YOU."

Even so, God didn't abandon or turn away from us. Just the opposite, He pursued us, and I sensed that pursuit over and over again. Someone would invite us to church. We wouldn't go, but it was like God was tapping us on the shoulder, saying, "Hey, remember me?" I remember one Christmas getting a package from my sister-in-law. She didn't normally send us a gift, and when I opened it, it was a Bible. My parents never quit talking about God and His control and goodness to us. They took every opportunity to put God in front of us. Then there were those times I'd see or hear about some wrongdoing and get mad because that person was "sinning." Immediately my conscience would be pricked because I knew I wasn't living right, either. And God continued to make the way and provide for us, even though we weren't paying any attention to Him and didn't pursue His provision or love.

I could absolutely feel God in these situations and others, but I refused to acknowledge and submit to Him. My attitude was, "I love You, Lord, and if I need You, I'll call You." You see, I thought my plan—to graduate from law school, get a good (no, actually great) job afterward, buy a big house in the "right" neighborhood, drive a new car, and have only the best, in-style clothing—was perfect. After all, everything was going well, so I certainly didn't need to consult the Lord about my life. Every accomplishment fed my ME syndrome. And as my plans seemingly kept falling into place, instead of thanking God for His help, my thinking was, *Whew, I'm doing a pretty good job at my life, thank you very much.*

After graduation, I got a job at a good law firm and right away was able to work in the areas I liked: litigation, bankruptcy, and business transactions. Along with the new job, Jeff and I built a new house. Through it all, God continued to pursue me, but my arm's length, consistent response was, "Hey, God, I'm doing good. And, oh yeah, I love You."

And then it happened. It's as though God said to me, "Enough is enough, Tami. If you are not willing to give Me your attention, I'm going to make you give Me your attention." And He certainly did.

PAINFUL LESSONS

I started having anxiety and panic attacks. Acute anxiety

is difficult to describe, because it is not driven by rational thinking. My bouts of anxiety were related initially to my practicing law. I was absolutely terrified of making a mistake, even though I'd never had a problem with that. Here's how my anxiety would typically play out. I would go home at the end of a workday, and immediately my mind would start running back over my cases and details of individual files. I would think to myself, *What if "x" isn't accurate?* Or, *What if I put the wrong response date on a court document?* Second guessing was routine for *every* evening and weekend. *What if I missed a filing deadline?* Or, *What if there was additional case law or statutory law that I didn't uncover? What if I didn't present the best and strongest argument?* And the list would go on and on.

In short order I'd fixate on one of those "what-ifs," and then I'd proceed to obsess over it. The initial what-if would lead to another worse what-if and then another and another. And as I moved down the what-if path, I would get more and more anxious, frantic, irrational. It was awful. And even worse, once the cycle began, I couldn't control it. In fact, the more I tried to take control, the worse I got.

Each anxiety experience was absolutely painful but also infuriating because I felt like I had been so in control of things up to this point. My anxiety made me feel weak, helpless, stupid.

Needless to say, my problems with anxiety didn't affect just me alone. As my anxiety grew and consumed me, it directly impacted the most important person in my life, my precious husband. I disengaged emotionally from Jeff. I'd spend time with him, but I was trying so hard to control my anxious thoughts that my focus wasn't really on him, what he was saying, or even what we were doing together. I lost my appetite; I wasn't sleeping well. I was visibly tense much of the time.

Jeff had never experienced anxiety, so he did not understand what was going on with me. And, honestly, I didn't understand it either. If Jeff called me in the middle of my day, I seemed fine to him because when I was at the office I was in control and could take whatever action I felt was needed. My files were in front of me, I could work on letters and court documents, I could call opposing counsel about cases. So I didn't typically have anxiety there. But at night, that all changed. The courts and businesses were closed. I no longer felt like I was in control so my anxiety would kick in.

Jeff wanted to help me and to be supportive, but the irrational thinking and behavior that was becoming the norm for me frustrated him. And as my problems with anxiety grew, his frustration turned to anger.

One thing that helped to diffuse my anxiety was talking to someone I trusted. I'd try to explain what was making me panicked. That helped some of my bottled up, irrational think-ing get out. As I voiced my fearful and illogical thoughts and conclusions, I would actually recognize how crazy I sounded and the paranoid nature of that specific thinking. Unfortunately this was not a pleasant experience for the person on the listen-ing end, which was usually Jeff.

Many times, he'd tell me I was being irrational. And though I knew that was true, I couldn't grab on to that truth and use it to stop the anxiety. Other times in frustration and anger, Jeff would tell me to "just stop" or to "suck it up." This wasn't helpful at all. In fact, more often than not, it heightened my anxiety because I *wasn't* capable of stopping it.

At some point, my anxiety expanded to situations that had nothing to do with work. For example, I'd remember something wrong I had done in my past (sometimes ten or fifteen years before), and I'd review it in my head over and over. I'd obsess over the "sin," even though I had asked for forgiveness numer-ous times. Next thing you know, my what-if thinking would kick into gear. *What if someone found out the terrible thing I had done? How could I ever live with that? How would that affect the here and now?*

One Sunday afternoon Jeff and I were golfing and we went into the clubhouse to buy sports drinks and some cookies. On our way home, I realized the concession girl had not charged us enough for the cookies (she had miscalculated by a dollar).

Jeff urged me to let the mistake go, but I couldn't. Anxiety took over. I was totally panicked over the thought that I had sinned by not paying what was owed. After a couple of hours of anxiety, I ended up driving back to the golf course and taking a dollar into the concession stand. I explained what had happened and that I wanted to make it right. They looked at me like I was crazy, and I'm pretty sure they took my dollar just so I would leave.

As my anxiety continued to do a number on me, Jeff's and my relationship began to deteriorate and serious problems within our marriage began to crop up. I was miserable, and I'm pretty sure Jeff was too, but I still hadn't made the connection that I should be turning this over to God.

THE RIGHT ROAD

A few weekends later I attended an out-of-town Continuing Legal Education seminar. As I sat through session after session, reviewing new cases and current law, all the things I "could have" possibly done wrong seemed highlighted to me. My anxiety was in overdrive. When the seminar ended, I began the three-hour drive home feeling miserable and panicky. At some point I turned on the radio and came across a broadcast of a Christian women's conference. The speaker was talking about her lifelong struggle with overwhelming fear and how God had used it to get her attention and turn her focus back to Him. Her words pierced my heart. For the first time I realized how far I had allowed myself to fall away from God.

There I was, driving down Interstate 80, convicted—BIG TIME. I couldn't get home fast enough. Jeff was gone that weekend, and I remember so vividly driving into the garage, running into the house, and throwing myself on the floor in front of our couch. I was on my knees, crying and finally broken before God. Through tears and sobs I asked the Lord to forgive me and to help me get back where I needed to be—focused on Him, not me. I'll never forget the immediate feeling of peace and relief that followed.

Now, if I had my way, the rest of my story would be how I woke up the next day and the birds were singing and the sun was shining brighter than ever before and my anxiety was completely gone. What a dreamer I am! The truth is, my tearful talk with God was just a baby step down the right road. I hadn't become emotionally and spiritually bankrupt overnight. So, me righting my relationship with God was going to take effort, time, and commitment on my part.

Church was a big part of my turnaround. Jeff and I had started going back to church, and after my "living room exchange" with God, I wanted to get more involved, and I did. Being around other Christians gave me needed encouragement. Seeing how God was working in other people's lives gave me reassurance that He would work in mine, too.

I knew I needed to be taking in and applying God's Word. But at this point, my Bible reading was pretty sporadic. I would start and stop and then start again. It was slow going for quite a while. But I kept at it, and as a result I began growing closer to God, and I'm still on that journey today.

So what's the status of my anxiety now? Well, as much as I'd like to tell you it's completely gone, it's not. There are still times I struggle with anxiety. That's frustrating to me, because my relationship with the Lord is stronger than it's ever been. But I've come to the conclusion that my anxiety is there to serve a purpose. You see, God knows me better than anyone, and that means He is well aware of my shortcomings, especially that dark, selfish part of my heart. I truly believe that if God took away every twinge of anxiety, I would be tempted and most likely fall back into the same me-centric behavior and thinking of my past.

THROUGH TEARS AND SOBS I ASKED THE LORD TO FORGIVE ME.

The older I get the more I realize how far I am from perfect. So I'm trusting God in and through my circumstances. He knows what's best for me, and yes, that includes anxiety.

MY BIBLE ENGAGEMENT JOURNEY

I've come to realize over the past fifteen years, and most keenly in the last five years, just how important it is for me to be consistently engaging God's Word—that is, receiving, reflecting on, and responding to Scripture. (I'll repeat this description a few times throughout this book; it's that important.) Here's why: God speaks to us through His Word, the Bible. He's not some distant, far-off God we have to wonder about. He reveals Himself to us—His heart and His mind— through the Bible. That being the case, I want to make sure the time I spend in the Word is as personal with God, on a relational level, as I can make it. I also want my time in the Word, and in particular the way I apply it, to be as personal to me as possible. In other words, what should I be doing with what I hear from God?

I KNEW MY TIME IN THE WORD COULD, AND SHOULD, BE BETTER.

A few years back I had an "aha" moment: There isn't a one-size-fits-all way to meet with God, take in His Word, and put it into practice. I don't know why I didn't see this before, but I didn't. Instead, I had in my mind that *the* way I was supposed to engage the Bible must be like a pastor or a scholarly theologian. I had no real idea what that actually involved, but I was certain it had to be tedious and boring. Yet, I knew I was supposed to be reading my Bible. I knew I needed it, because, after all, it was God's Word. I knew the Bible was where I'd find instruction for how to live my life in a way that would be pleasing to God. So I kept at it.

I'd start reading the Bible for a stretch. Sometimes I'd even read every day for a couple of weeks, but then something would come up and I'd get pulled off course. I'd go for a few days, maybe a couple of weeks, and a similar cycle would start again. Not a best-case scenario. Still, even through these sporadic, half-hearted efforts, I was learning and picking things up here and there. Deep down, though, I knew my time in the Word could, and should, be better. I just wasn't sure what to do to make it better or to make it more exciting.

I have to say, the problem I was experiencing with my Bible reading had nothing to do with the Bible being too hard to read or understand, or the Bible being boring, or the Bible not being relevant, because *none of that is true.* The problem was with me and my heart and attitude.

I was a Christ-follower, I went to church, and, if you asked, I would tell you I wanted to know God more and better. And I did want that—provided it didn't require too much commitment or too much cutting into my personal time. Getting to know God better through His Word wasn't yet a priority.

But God didn't give up on me. As I got more involved in church and then started working at Back to the Bible in 2000, the clear message to me was that God's Word had to be a priority in my life. I knew I had to do better. One day, I said to myself, *"Enough is enough. Get up and do this."* And right there, I made the commitment that I would be obedient to God's call for me to get to know Him better through His Word. I didn't realize it at the time, but this decision would be a life-changing one for me.

So with obedience as my motivation and driver, I began reading my Bible using a reading plan. I didn't really care for the structure, but I read that way for a while. I was learning and growing little by little, but I still wasn't to the place where my mom was—being joyful and looking forward to opening the Bible every day.

A FRESH APPROACH

One day I received some book samples at work, and one of the books was a chronological Bible. Eventually, I looked through it and was intrigued because it wasn't arranged like a traditional Bible, book by book. Instead, it was the entire Bible arranged in chronological order. So if I was reading from 1 Samuel 24 about Saul chasing David through the wilderness, inserted in the story line would be the corresponding psalm (in this case Psalm 57) that David wrote at that time. Additionally, many of the books of the Bible were in a different order than I was used to. The more I read, the more things started to fit together and make sense.

In just a couple of weeks, I was enjoying my Bible reading like never before. I wanted to know what happened next in God's great story and why. This was a *huge* step forward for me, not only because I was engaging the Bible like never before, but also because the chronological approach showed me the significance and importance of the Old Testament. Up to this point I had convinced myself that the Old Testament was dry and boring, and I'd done my best to avoid it. Today, the Old Testament is my favorite place to spend time in the Word.

It had been about five years from the time I made that commitment to be obedient about being in the Word until I discovered the chronological Bible. And when I look back, I am surprised and amazed how these changes impacted my life. During those five years, God was at work in my heart, and although I can't tell you when or where, my focus became more and more about God and living for Him. For the first time, I really got it. My attitude, my motivation, where I was in my relationship with God and spiritually—it was all the result of the time I had spent in God's Word.

EXTERNAL EVIDENCE

During this same period, Back to the Bible began conducting nationwide surveys on the Bible-reading habits of Christians. The surveys were designed to answer the question: "Why do so many people own Bibles but rarely read them?" The results were eye-opening but also meaningful for me personally, because the research showed exactly what I had experienced—that consistently being in the Word four or more times a week is a key factor to living a godly life and growing spiritually (see the appendix for more information on the survey findings). I was excited, both about my own experience and also about what the research was telling us.

MY TIME IN THE WORD WAS GIVING ME A PEACE AND CONTENTMENT THAT I TRULY HAD NOT EXPERIENCED BEFORE.

Then in 2008 I started writing a daily blog for Back to the Bible that was focused on Scripture. The blog is called *Powered by 4*, and as the voice of the blog, I read the assigned passage for the day and then write about what God impressed on my heart from that passage. The purpose of the blog is to encourage and help people engage God's Word—to receive, reflect on, and respond to Scripture—four or more times a week. So to help others (and myself) engage, I typically conclude each blog with some sort of application question or call to action based on that day's Scripture passage.

When I started writing these daily blog posts, I had no idea the task I had signed up for. It was a *huge* commitment. But more importantly, the blog caused me to modify the approach I was using for my personal Bible reading. Because I was now in an encourager role and prompting people to not just read but engage the Word, I had to do the same in order to be authentic in my own application of Scriptures.

I quickly discovered I hadn't always been reflecting and responding when I'd been spending personal time in the Word. I'd assumed I was, but sometimes I had just been reading (receiving), and leaving it at that.

I am grateful for *Powered by 4*, because what I thought was already a good time with God and His Word got even better. And as the weeks and then months came and went, I realized one morning that I had taken a step or two forward in my spiritual growth. God was showing me so much, and my time in the Word was giving me a peace and contentment that I truly had not experienced before. God is so amazing. Engaging my Bible had shifted from something I needed to do, to just being part of who I am as a follower of Christ.

So, what has God shown me, and what have I learned from all that I've experienced? A lot. Here are a few key points:

- **God is in control.** It took me a long time to admit this. Deep down I knew God was in control, but I was determined to be the boss of me. I was so sure I knew what was best. I was so sure I could handle anything that came my way. Well, I was *so* wrong, and my defiant, sinful attitude caused me pain and heartache that I could have avoided had I simply submitted to God.

- **I can have joy in all circumstances.** I may not be happy about everything happening in my life, but with God and His Word as my foundation, I can still be joyful. Happiness is an emotion that comes and goes with circumstances. Being joyful is an attitude that comes when I rely on and trust in God and the promises found only in His Word.

+ **My job is to serve the Lord.** For so many years, my goals were wrapped up in what I thought would make me happy—money and having things. But no matter how much I had, I never felt satisfied. After turning back to the Lord, my thinking changed and I realized that God has put me here on this earth to serve Him. Starting each day with serving God as my goal allows me to face my day with joy no matter what the day may hold.

+ **God-focus, not me-focus.** I want God to be my focus. I *need* God to be my focus. Even so, this continues to be a struggle for me. If I'm not intentional about my focus, before I know it, that "it's all about me" thinking creeps in, and God is pushed into a secondary position. As a result, my spiritual life suffers and things in my life start to unravel.

+ **God will never abandon me.** I am so thankful for God's love and faithfulness. He was there for me, although I didn't acknowledge Him, during the years I was determined to do my own thing. He was there through my dad's and mom's cancer battles and deaths. He was there through a miscarriage and my husband's cancer and ongoing autoimmune problems. And He's here right now, walking with me and guiding me.

RESPONDING TO GOD'S WORD

My favorite way to engage Scripture today is what I call "Take It In, Live It Out." (And I really mean *today*, because as I grow in my relationship with God, the way I like to meet with God and take in His Word might change or grow as well!) I start by reading a Bible passage completely through. Then I go back and read it again, but this time I stop after each verse and do my best to consider every thought, command, or example that I can see. I do that by asking myself a few questions, such as:

+ How does "x" apply to me? How might I put "x" into practice in my life? What specific steps would I need to take?

+ Is my heart in the same place as the writer of the passage? Why or why not? How do I get my heart to that place? How do I maintain this attitude?

+ How can I use this passage to help me as I go forward?

So let's say I've selected Matthew 7:24-25 for my time with the Lord. The first thing I'd do is read the passage all the way through, just to get a sense of the substance of the passage. At this point, I'm not reading with a particular focus or goal.

> [24]*Everyone then who hears these words of mine and does them will be like a wise man who built his house on the rock.* [25]*And the rain fell, and the floods came, and the winds blew and beat on that house, but it did not fall, because it had been founded on the rock.*
> —Matthew 7:24-25

Then, I'd go back to verse 24 and read it again, but now with the intent of considering the verse in phrases and also as a whole. That's where asking myself questions comes in. So for verse 24, one of the first questions I'd ask is, "Am I hearing (taking in) God's Word and living according to it?" Then I'd ask, "Why or why not?" And if my answer isn't a confident "Yes, I am," then I need to answer these questions: "What can I do to change this? What do I need to do to improve my taking in and living out of God's Word?"

Then I'd move on to the second half of the passage and consider, "When has the rain fallen or the winds blown hard in my life? How did I respond? And what does my response show me about my grounding and my foundation?" From there I'd ask myself, "Is my spiritual foundation God and His Word? Could I have a stronger foundation, or what do I need to do to get a stronger foundation?"

This approach allows me to go as deep as I want and to spend as much time as I like or need on brief portions of

Scripture. Plus, the questions I ask and how I'm considering these segments of Scripture are unique to me. I like that freedom and the fact that I am able to apply verses to my life and my situation that very day. I always come away with something to work on—something to put into practice—that will move me closer to God and help me grow spiritually.

A TAKE IT IN, LIVE IT OUT RESPONSE TO PSALM 63:1

Psalm 63 is one of my favorite psalms, and it works well with a Take It In, Live It Out approach. I've worked through verse 1 below so you can see my thinking, some of the "stops" I took while considering it, and how I responded. Once you look over what I've done, I invite you to engage the first eight verses of Psalm 63 (or another Scripture passage) yourself.

> *Oh God, you are my God; earnestly I seek you; my soul thirsts for you; my flesh faints for you, as in a dry and weary land where there is no water.*
> —Psalm 63:1

"Oh God, you are my God." This is my first stopping point, because there's plenty to consider in this short six-word phrase. As I read this, two questions immediately come to mind: *Do I truly believe that God is "my God"?* and *What exactly does "you are my God" mean for me?* Sometimes I will just think through my responses to a Scripture passage. But other times I'll write down my thoughts, so I can later read how what I saw fits together, or ponder the many things God has shown me.

My response: *Do I truly believe that God is "my God"?* Yes, I do believe that You, God, are mine, because Your Word tells me that over and over again. Sometimes, though, it's hard for me to fully grasp the concept that You are mine and that I am Yours because there are so many people out there, and I'm just one little speck, one little blip, on a *huge* radar screen.

What does "you are my God" mean for me? This very moment, it means that I know You, God. I know that I can talk with You, that I can meet with You in Your Word, that I can call out to You for help, that I can look to You for guidance. You being "my God" means I feel secure and at peace, because I know You personally, and I know that You are watching over me. Thank you, God. I love You.

What are some examples of God being "my God"? How has God shown me that He is "my God"? Yes, God has shown me over and over again, through both big and little circumstances, that He is my God. The biggest demonstration was the entire experience with Jeff's cancer. I was afraid and uncertain. I wanted to be there for Jeff. I wanted to help him however I could, but I didn't really know what to do. I shared all this with God and told Him that I was entrusting Jeff to Him. That was a hard step for me, but I knew I had to take it, because I did believe that God was "my God." And God responded without missing a beat. He supplied me with every ounce of strength, hope, love, and "my God" encouragement that I needed.

I love how God shows me that He's "my God" through the small things. One example of a small thing is how God seems to smile on me when it comes to finding great parking spots. Almost everywhere I drive, there will be an up-close parking spot waiting for me. It's a practical reminder of how God provides for me. So every time it happens, I smile and immediately shoot up a "thank-you, God" prayer.

"Earnestly I seek you." *Does this describe me? Am I earnestly seeking God? And, is it enough?* Yes, I do seek God. But I'm not confident that I always "earnestly" seek Him. I'm absolutely sincere about meeting God in His Word. So I do believe my attitude is earnest. The question I have is, am I spending enough time in the Word? I could do more, so I hesitate to affirm, at least where time is concerned, that I'm totally earnest.

"My soul thirsts for you; my flesh faints for you, as in a dry and weary land where there is no water." This is my favorite part of verse 1. It's so descriptive that it's easy to feel how much David desires God. Every person has experienced thirst. There's nothing quite like drinking a cold glass of water when your mouth is incredibly dry and you feel like you're dying of thirst. And we've probably all seen soil that is bone-dry and in need of water. The dirt is cracked and split open because it desperately needs water. And when water comes, the soil immediately absorbs it and is replenished and beautiful.

Does my experience with thirst—like parched soil desperate for water—describe my heart and my attitude when it comes to my relationship with God? Why or why not? Most of the time it does. But if I'm honest, not always. If I miss a day or maybe two of reading my Bible, I'm amazed at how my "thirsting" for God starts to dissipate. So I need to be tuned in to that and careful to guard my time with God and His Word.

So what is it that hinders my relationship with God? So often for me, it's just busyness. I overbook, over commit, over plan, and the next thing I know I've pushed my Bible reading and time with God aside. Or, maybe something happens that gets me distracted. Maybe I'm just being lazy. Whatever the case, if I don't read the Bible for a few days, my thinking tends toward, *No big deal. I'll get back to my routine with God when I have time.* That's dangerous because it can lead into a major backslide.

How do I maintain this desire for God? The best way for me to maintain and grow my desire for God is to be intentional about meeting with Him daily. The more I immerse myself in His Word, the more God shows me about Himself and how to live a better life, which makes me want to keep coming back.

POST-PSALM 63 THOUGHTS

So that's how I worked through verse 1 of Psalm 63, and hopefully, you've gotten a good feel for the Take It In, Live It Out approach. As you can see, depending on the questions you ask yourself and the depth of what you consider, you can spend a little or a lot of time on even one verse. This approach is so flexible that even if you're short on time, you can easily get in some Bible engagement, and then you can keep mulling over whatever questions come to mind as you go through your day.

I vary from day to day on how much time I spend and how in-depth I go on verses. Some days I'll really focus on a single verse and just stay there, taking in all that the Lord shows me. Other days, I'll read an entire chapter, and then go back and focus on one or two key things that stood out for me. I like that freedom because it allows me to tailor my time in the Word with how I believe God is leading me on a particular day.

So now it's your turn try the Take It In, Live It Out approach with Psalm 63:1-8. I hope you enjoy this approach as much as I do, and that the time you spend in Psalm 63 will be meaningful. If you're not quite sure where to start or what to consider, I've included some sample questions below that you can choose from to help you. Have fun making Psalm 63 uniquely applicable to you.

SAMPLE QUESTIONS TO HELP YOU ENGAGE GOD'S WORD

Primary (or Big Picture) Questions or Considerations

+ What can I take away from this verse or passage?

+ What is God revealing to me through this passage?

+ What is God trying to teach me through this passage?

+ What does God desire for me to do based on this passage?

+ How can I use what I've read going forward?

Secondary (More Specific) Questions You Might Consider

+ Does this verse describe me or my behavior? If yes, how did I get to this point? If not, why?

+ Am I like the writer with regard to attitude or actions?

+ Am I living what I'm reading?

+ How can I be more like the writer or the person about whom I'm reading? How specifically do I do that?

+ How did the person in the passage get to where they were spiritually?

+ Do I have any personal experience with, or examples of, what I'm reading about? If so, what was my response or reaction compared to the text?

+ Was there an approach, tactic, or method used that I might be able to put into practice?

+ What does this verse tell me about God generally? What God expects from me? What God likes or dislikes?

+ What does this verse show me about my relationship with God? My need for God?

+ What does this verse reveal about me and my nature?

+ What does this verse reveal about the past?
  The present? The future? The world? Sin?

+ How does this speak to my current situation?
  My heart? Thinking? Actions? Emotions? My approach?

+ Do I truly believe what I'm reading? Why or why not?

+ What does this show me about dealing with people?
  Conflict? Money?

+ How can I improve where I'm at spiritually?

+ What can I do to grow in my relationship with God?

+ What should I be thanking God for?

+ Are there actions I need to take based on the verse or
  passage? Do I need to pray? Confess? Ask for forgiveness?
  Thank God? Tell others? Help someone? Get involved?

+ What promises can I claim from this verse/passage?

As you speak to God, asking Him to reveal Himself through His Word, open the ears of your heart to hear His voice speaking to *you*.

"I was very much riding on

the coattails of my sisters,

and subconsciously, I was

trying to make my parents happy.

I was doing what was expected of me.

I think I also knew that

when I left home, things would

change significantly for me.

I just kind of felt like I had to

bide my time and be a good child

and obey the rules."

CHAPTER 2

FILLING THAT GOD-SHAPED HOLE IN OUR HEARTS:

CARLY'S STORY

*"She attended that first AA meeting, with Craig, drunk.
Sitting beside him, silent, she hung her head low. When she heard
God mentioned several times, she shot Craig a look that said,
"You've got to be kidding, right?" It was then that, although
she'd never been able to admit it, she realized she hated God."*

AS WE SAT IN big overstuffed chairs at the local coffee shop, Carly told me a bit about herself. "When I left my parent's home, I cut off my hair. I pierced my ears. I did whatever I wanted to do. People viewed me as individualistic, funky, whatever, and I fed off of that. I'm the girl who walks in the room and everybody knows I'm there. I mean, hello, look at that hair!"

I smiled because that's pretty much what I thought the first time I met her. There was no doubt she wanted to be noticed, and although I didn't voice it, it did cross my mind, *That girl has some unresolved issues.*

That was almost five years ago, and at the time I had no idea who Carly was, her background, or that she and I would become friends in the future.

CARLY'S STORY

Carly, the youngest of five siblings, all girls, was raised in a strong Christian home. When she was five, she asked Jesus into her heart while waiting at a stoplight in the car with her family. Growing up, Carly's parents had clear expectations for their girls (Carly's exact words were "high, high expectations"). She and her sisters knew how they were to act and what they were to do.

Carly described her oldest sister as the beautiful one, and her other sister as an outstanding athlete. Wanting to be recognized on her own, Carly jumped head first into pretty much every activity she could. She played multiple sports, was the student council president, participated in choir, band, and speech, and was highly involved in church.

Knowing that Carly was a Christian during her teen years, I asked her if she was reading the Word at that time. "Not much. Looking back, I would have described my relationship with God as being very solid. But I was very much riding on the coattails of my sisters, and subconsciously, I was trying to make my parents happy. I was doing what was expected of me. I think I also knew that when I left home, things would change significantly for me. I just kind of felt like I had to bide my time and be a good child and obey the rules."

Bide my time. I had to ask Carly what she meant. Did she have some idea of doing something else? Carly said it boiled down to wanting to do what *she* wanted. She simply wanted control of her own life. I couldn't help but think, *Been there, done that.*

Although her parents preferred that she attend a Christian college, Carly chose a state university. Her parents did insist, however, that she be involved in some sort of college ministry. Carly agreed, but not wholeheartedly. And shortly after moving onto campus, Carly was already taking a first big step away from her parents and down a dangerous, slippery slope.

CRITICAL CHOICES

"I was on campus just three weeks before I got drunk for the first time," Carly told me. "I was really torn between two lifestyles that year. I was involved in Campus Crusade for Christ, and I kept that group of friends separate from my partying friends. I was thinking, *Nobody knows me, I can do anything I want, and nobody's going to run home and tell my parents what I've done, so I'm going to do what I want to do—period.* And I did."

Before long, Carly was dating a senior, partying with him and friends, and smoking pot. "We'd go out and get trashed, and I'd have no guilt about it." She still was going to church, but her attendance waned as she continued to do more and more of her own thing. Not surprisingly, the Word was not part of her life.

I REMEMBER CRYING AND YELLING, 'JUST YELL AT ME OR SOMETHING,' BUT THEY WOULDN'T DO IT.

"No, no, no," she told me. "I knew enough from growing up in church. I knew the stories of the Bible. I could talk to anybody and pretty much pull the wool over their eyes. I was part of a college group at church, and then I started seeing people there that I had partied with the night before. I thought, *I don't need to come here anymore because these people are a bunch of hypocrites.*" Carly's quick laugh at the memory confirmed that the irony was not lost on her.

Back then it was all about Carly controlling Carly. But the more she did whatever she wanted, the more life spiraled out of control. By the end of her freshman year, Carly was sleeping with her boyfriend and using cocaine. She flunked out of school, and her freewheeling lifestyle continued.

"Then I got pregnant. I was twenty-two. My child's dad had a nice truck and a lot of drugs, and that's pretty much how we hooked up," Carly explained. "We weren't together long, and three days after we broke up I found out I was pregnant."

Carly was frightened. She didn't know what to do. But for the first time she was able to admit to herself that she had a drinking problem. Still, she didn't want her family to know anything.

With nowhere else to turn, though, Carly finally mustered up the courage to tell her parents she was pregnant. "I was terrified, because I didn't know what their reaction would be. What happened shocked me. My family welcomed me home with open arms. Their demonstration of grace to me was huge. I remember crying and yelling, 'Just yell at me or something,' but they wouldn't do it."

Through the gracious embrace of her family, God reminded Carly of His presence. Then she was met by another gracious encounter. A day after reaching out to the church she once attended, she received a phone call. "This lady called and told me, 'Hey, I've been in your situation, and I'd love to just sit down and talk to you.'"

Carly accepted the invitation, and she and Susan became fast friends. Susan became a source of strength to Carly, and gave her the courage to return to church. "It was really horrifying for me to walk into church that first time because I had this big belly and no ring on my finger. I was fairly certain that everybody in the whole place was looking right at me. I don't remember what that first sermon was all about, but I know it was directed exactly toward me." Another chuckle revealed Carly's ability to take herself lightly.

With Carly's return to church and her staying away from alcohol, things seemed better, even all right. But in reality, her baby was about to arrive and there was a long, rough road ahead. "Brianna was born, and she was such a miracle," Carly said. "Her birth had a huge impact on me. But I still had a big chip on my shoulder as far as allowing people to help me or admitting I even needed help."

DESTRUCTIVE DECISION

Carly had not fully addressed her drinking problem, and one night her resolve broke. She went out with friends and got wasted. That one night turned into several nights. Eventually, Carly's use of alcohol became constant.

Debra, a woman at church, had been mentoring Carly. One day she approached Carly, pointed at her heart, and said, "There's something wrong." Carly was taken aback. Debra continued, "This, right here, is not where it should be. I don't know what it is, but there's something wrong."

As Carly had become accustomed to doing, she lied. Although her life had spiraled out of control during the six months she'd been drinking, she told the woman that she was fine. But the truth kept knocking at Carly's door.

Carly had been singing for her congregation's children's church, and she was often hung over. A guy who played in the band with her approached her between services. Getting up-close, face to face, Craig asked, "What are you doing? You're drunk."

"No, I'm not."

Craig pressed. "Don't lie to me, Carly. I've been watching you, and you are an alcoholic."

Cornered, Carly retorted, "You don't know anything about me. Get away. Just leave me alone. I don't want to talk to you."

Craig had no plans of leaving Carly alone. He went outside and brought back a book from Alcoholics Anonymous. "Here," he said, handing it to her. "I want you to read this."

Carly protested. "You can't give this to me. We're in church. What if somebody sees it? "

Undeterred, Craig answered, "Carly, you've got a problem. You need to read this, and we need to talk."

As Carly recalled that morning for me, she said, "You know, that week was a really tough, tough week. I drank every single night until I couldn't stay awake anymore, but Craig finally convinced me to go to an AA meeting with him."

She attended that first AA meeting, with Craig, drunk. Sitting beside him, silent, she hung her head low. When she heard God mentioned several times, she shot Craig a look that said, "You've got to be kidding, right?" It was then that, although she'd never been able to admit it, she realized she hated God. Religion had always been something she was supposed to do. She was furious that even in the place Craig had brought her to get sober, it was still all about God.

"I hadn't made the connection, yet, that God was how I would get sober," Carly reflected.

I took a deep breath and leaned in. "Carly, I have to be honest with you. It's shocking to hear you say you hated God. Why did you choose those specific words?" She gave me a little smile and a knowing look.

"It felt like every moment of my life came crashing down then—the choices I had made in my life prior to ever taking a drink, the constant feeling that I had to make everybody happy, that I was never good enough, that I hated my parents, that I hated my family, that I hated everybody around me. But more than anything,, I hated myself."

"But how was God responsible for that?" I had to ask.

Carly, true to form, shot me another honest response. "He just was," she said with another chuckle. "If I really and truly believed He was God, then why would He allow—and this is from a completely selfish standpoint— why would He allow my life to be what it was, if He really loved me? And if He really loved me, why did I hurt so bad?" She added, "You've heard people talk about a God-shaped hole in their hearts? I realize now that mine was gaping, and I tried to fill it with everything. Everything."

I pressed on. "Okay. So you're saying you were dying to have a relationship with God, but you wanted God to be the God you had in mind. On your terms."

"Absolutely," Carly said. "I wanted to check in on Sunday mornings and maybe at mealtime, and then have God just leave me alone other than making sure things went the way I wanted them to." Carly wrestled to articulate why it was she hated God. Then she admitted, "I had messed everything up. I needed someone else to blame."

At that time in her life, Carly was angry—at God, at Craig, at herself. Thankfully, she chose not to walk away. She gave Alcoholics Anonymous a try, and worked through the steps of the program while God was working on her heart.

A CHANGED HEART

"The first steps of AA connect, or reconnect, you to God," Carly explained. "They call you to give up control of your life, because you're not really doing a bang up job of that anyway, you know? It's important to believe that God can and will change your life. The middle steps are doing an inventory, basically, where you confront everything in your life—your past, your present. It's not fun sitting down with your sponsor and telling him secrets you swore no one would ever know."

I loved that Carly didn't recite a memorized checklist to me as she explained the AA steps. Instead, she pulled me in, and let me in, to all she went through.

She described finally confessing everything to God. Sitting in the middle of her living room floor, sobbing and rocking back and forth, she implored Him, "Come in. Take over my life. You know all of this—the last thirty years and how I treated my relationship with You. I'm done. It's Yours." She visualized Jesus beside her and felt his loving arms wrapped around her. From that moment on, Carly's view of God changed completely. God was no longer the One who wanted to smite her if she sinned, but the One who wanted to be in relationship with her. "You know," she reflected, "as I sit here today, if I had to name a moment of salvation, that would be it for me."

I could so relate to Carly's living room surrender to God. I too had recommitted my life to God after quite a few years of calling my own shots. Surrendering is the first step, but to grow in our relationship with the Lord, we have to be in His Word.

LISTENING TO GOD

"I've always been a reader," Carly said. "I am constantly reading something. So when Craig, who ended up being my sponsor, got me a Recovery Bible, I read that more than anything else. I couldn't get enough of it. I started in the gospels, focusing on the text in red letters—the words Jesus spoke. I knew that was how I was going to gain an understanding of who Jesus is." The words about Jesus' character and grace and love and mercy came alive for Carly. She said it was like reading the Bible for the first time.

IT'S IMPORTANT TO BELIEVE THAT GOD CAN AND WILL CHANGE YOUR LIFE.

Carly even found a fresh way to pray. "I've never been good at praying, so I started journaling my prayers. I knew that if I just kept my pen moving, I would get out what I needed to get out." The process, she said, kept her mind from wandering. Once she started writing her prayers, she was able to look back and recognize how God was answering them—in ways she might have expected and ways she hadn't!

Carly had already told me how important the gospels were to her, but I asked which verses or stories in the Bible were particularly meaningful to her. The psalms were significant for her when she was initially getting sober, and she also mentioned Isaiah chapters 40 to 42, as well as the prophet's announcement of Jeremiah 29:11: "For I know the plans I have for you . . ." But she found herself going to the book of James most often—a book that encourages us to live a holy life, not saying one thing and doing another. With a little smile and a laugh, Carly told me, "I love James, and hate James, at the same time."

WHAT WE CAN LEARN FROM CARLY'S STORY

I'm a firm believer in considering and thinking through things I read, hear, and see. So after my time with Carly, I asked myself, *What can I learn from Carly's story?* And, *What happened with Carly that I need to be tuned in to and watching out for?*

+ **Choices are critical.** Carly's story shows how even one seemingly small choice can derail us (for Carly, going out with friends and getting drunk that one night after staying away from alcohol for months). One decision can change our life—for good or for bad.

+ **Living for "self" is dangerous.** This came through loud and clear through Carly's rebellious actions and her choice to live according to her will. It was definitely the most powerful message for me. When we make "self" the center of our life—when we allow our thinking to be all about us, our wants, our needs—we will never be satisfied, because we aren't in a right relationship with God (and can't be in this state). If we're not careful, it's easy to fall back into this attitude and way of operating. I want to avoid going down that road again, and the best way I can guard against that happening is to consistently be in God's Word.

+ **God will get our attention.** Why is it that so many times God has to get our attention? Why do we have to hit rock bottom before we'll surrender to Him? It sure would be easier and a whole lot more pleasant if we'd just recognize God for who He is and live accordingly. It seems to happen that way for some people. But it didn't happen that way for Carly, and I'm sorry to say, it didn't happen that way for me either. For too long I was focused on me and what I wanted, and I was definitely set on being in control. Yes, I had received Christ as my Savior, but over time I had pushed God into a dark corner in the basement of my heart. It's no wonder that God taking back His space was painful.

+ **Relationship—not religion.** When Carly finally surrendered to God, crying out to Him as she sat on the floor of her living room, she said that was the moment her view of God changed "to someone who wanted to have a relationship with me." Her words and the way she described the situation jolted my heart. I thought to myself, *Yes, I've been there, and you are so right.* Up to this point, Carly had pretty much been doing Christian activities and reading her Bible with a "duty" mindset, or she was doing it to please other people. Her perception of God was not up-close and personal, or even loving or caring.

RESPONDING TO GOD'S WORD

After Carly surrendered to God, she found she had a huge desire to read her Bible. "It was almost like I couldn't get enough of it," she said. She soon discovered that the best thing for her to do was to simply sit down and read. She knew praying was important too, but she didn't feel she was a strong pray-er. "I've never been good at praying, so I started journaling a lot and journaling my prayers. I knew that if I just kept my pen moving, I'd get out what I needed to get out."

Carly walked me through her routine. "I always like to journal after I read. I spend a few minutes praying before I start to read the Bible. I pray something like, 'Lord, this is what I'm going to read tonight. Point out to me what I need to see, or point me somewhere else if that's where You want me to go.' Then I'll read. I don't have predetermined, set amounts to read. I read until I don't want to read anymore. Sometimes it's a chapter. Sometimes it's a whole book. Then after I'm done reading, I journal my thoughts, which for me, come out in prayer form. Typically it's about something that stuck out to me. Sometimes I'll underline as I'm reading or jot down a word or two so I can include that in my prayer journaling. But there are other times when what I journal doesn't center around my Scripture reading. It's more about what's going on in my life. I don't know if what I do is the best method, but it's working for me."

I was intrigued, because I'd never considered combining journaling and prayer as a way to help me grow closer to God. Plus, I'm not a natural "journaler" (though I must say that plenty of people have tried to guilt, badger, and pretty much assure me that if I'm not journaling or wanting to journal, I couldn't possibly go to heaven!—just kidding). I don't consider myself a particularly good pray-er either. Oh, I pray every day, but I'm definitely not a diligent "prayer warrior" like some people I know. The bottom line is, there's plenty of room for improvement in my prayer life. That being the case, trying Carly's prayer journaling method hit me as being a little scary and a bit of a challenge.

AFTER I'M DONE READING, I JOURNAL MY THOUGHTS, WHICH FOR ME, COME OUT IN PRAYER FORM.

Carly said the book of James is especially helpful and meaningful to her, so I thought it good to join with Carly and prayer journal through James. It is only five short chapters, and it's packed full of things for us to use and put into practice every single day. Plus, I've included my very first attempt at prayer journaling on three verses so you can see what I did. NOTE: *There are no right or wrong ways to prayer journal.* Make it your own and just talk to God in writing.

TAMI'S PRAYER JOURNAL: JAMES 4:1-3

"What causes quarrels and what causes fights among you? Is it not this, that your passions are at war within you? You desire and do not have, so you murder. You covet and cannot obtain, so you fight and quarrel. You do not have, because you do not ask. You ask and do not receive, because you ask wrongly, to spend it on your passions."

—James 4:1-3

Lord, it's hard for me to admit my weaknesses about wanting "things." Deep down I know that having an iPad, an iPhone, the right brand of jeans, the newest hairstyle, or whatever, won't really change things, and I'm not even sure what it is that I think I need to change. Yet I let myself go there anyway. I know it's not productive—wait,

I know it's wrong—but there's this part of me that likes having what I want because it makes me feel good, at least for a little while. Plus, there's a pride thing going on, too. It makes me feel good (in a warped kind of way) when I can show others how fortunate I am to have "x"— whatever that is at the time. I know it's pretty pathetic. So, Lord, I need your help.

It's funny because, You know, God, that there was a point where what I "had" was the driving force for me. And I thought I had overcome that. But honestly, it's still there, hanging out in the background. Thank You that I've made progress, but my wants are still pulling at me and affecting my actions and thoughts. So God, would you help me focus on You and Your Word? Would you help me be content because I have You? You are more import- ant than anything. Would you help me continue to do more to serve You and help others?

God, You are life. Please help me do a better job of staying in alignment with You. As I've realized yet again today, I can't do this (I can't do anything, really) alone. I love You.

POST-PRAYER JOURNALING THOUGHTS

When I first tried prayer journaling, it wasn't like anything I imagined. It was much better! You see, I hadn't relished the thought of my first attempt at prayer journaling. In fact, I had done a pretty good job of convincing myself it was going to be boring. I was absolutely wrong. Let me explain.

My plan was to read and then prayer journal on the first twelve verses of James 4. So I read the verses a couple of times and then picked up my pen to start writing. I had it in my head that I would write a simple sentence or two on each verse as my prayer, and end up with a paragraph of mini prayers. But that's not what happened at all. I had made the decision to be honest and tell God, in writing, exactly what came into my mind concerning these verses. Two things happened. As I started to write, a lot more ended up on my paper than I expected because I was being very free. And, I realized that I only wanted to journal on the first three verses because they touched on one issue, and I had plenty to discuss with God right there.

I spent about ten minutes writing, and when I finished, there was no doubt I had had a good, honest conversation with God. Something about writing out what I was thinking and feeling brought more depth to the conversation for me. So much so that I continued to contemplate my "prayer" for a couple of days, which isn't always the case when I read and spend time with God in my typical manner.

Will I continue to prayer journal? Most definitely. Will this now be my primary way of taking in God's Word and spending time with Him? Probably not, or maybe I should say, not yet. I do plan to include prayer journaling in my routine going forward, especially when I'm struggling with an issue, and also to add some variety to my talks with God.

So no matter where you're at spiritually—a frequent Bible reader, never really read the Bible, not a good pray-er, not a good writer, you name it—try prayer journaling. Take it a step at a time and see where you end up. I'm confident you won't regret it!

"I was a mess," Ginger said,

"so I flew across the country

to my aunt and uncle's."

Ginger paused for a moment.

"I remember sitting at their

kitchen table that first night

talking about life and

spiritual things. And that's when

all that I had learned and heard

about God and Jesus

finally made sense to me."

CHAPTER 3

GOD WON'T GIVE UP ON YOU:

GINGER'S STORY

*"I knew with all my heart, soul, mind—everything within my being—
that what I was doing was wrong, totally wrong. But the hurt and my
anger toward Christians was controlling me. I started going to the bars
with Tim, all the while getting further and further away from God.
I knew I was sinning but didn't stop. In fact, I moved in with Tim."*

GINGER AND I HAVE been close friends for many
years. So as we settled down in Ginger's living room with our
favorite beverage, Diet Pepsi, in hand, I wasn't expecting to
learn many new things about her. What I didn't realize is all
the second, third, and fourth chances she had experienced in
her spiritual journey.

When Ginger and her husband, Tim, reached their fifties, they felt God's call to serve Him full time. That was scary for them because Tim had worked in the tire industry his entire life, Ginger was the principal of their church's Christian school, and their youngest son, Brodie, was just starting high school. Even so, Tim and Ginger began looking into going overseas as missionaries. Within two years of feeling that first call to serve, Tim, Ginger, and Brodie sold their possessions and were on their way to Africa, leaving behind their jobs and family. It was a huge change, but they loved it.

Tim and Ginger ended up spending about ten years on the ground doing missionary work in Africa. Brodie spent part of the first year with them, and then returned to the United States to finish his senior year of high school and go on to college. Tim's work skills made him a perfect fit to head up all maintenance for the mission, and Ginger's administrative gifting was put to full use working with churches, pastors, and schools. After a few years in Africa, Ginger accepted the position of Field Director for Central Africa for the mission. Today, Ginger and Tim are living in the United States, with Ginger overseeing mission work being done in Africa and traveling there several times a year. They are heavily involved in their local church and passionate about helping others know Christ.

GINGER'S STORY

Ginger was raised in a Christian home. When she was five, she went forward at a children's revival night at church and was baptized the following Sunday. She considered herself a "good girl"—until she hit her teen years, that is.

Ginger bluntly told me, "Rebellious, drinking, and dating guys who weren't Christians is how I would describe my teenage years." So it wasn't a big surprise to find out that Ginger got married to a not-so-nice guy when she was eighteen and had already left him by the time she was twenty-one, because he was involved in drugs and other unhealthy things.

"I was a mess," Ginger said, "so I flew across the country to my aunt and uncle's." Ginger paused for a moment. "I remember sitting at their kitchen table that first night talking about life and spiritual things. And that's when all that I had learned and heard about God and Jesus finally made sense to me. That evening I truly asked Christ to be my Savior."

Over the next six months Ginger tried to work things out with her marriage, but her unsaved husband didn't like the new Christ-centered Ginger. Turning her life over to Christ had changed her from the inside out. She was excited about God's Word, loved going to church, and wanted to grow and learn more.

Ginger's eyes lit up as she described her new life. "I was

reading the Bible every day, involved in a Bible study for ladies, and I was at church every single time the doors were open. I was starving to know more about God and so grateful for His grace for me. I had a strong desire to learn more about God's Word, so I started checking out different Bible colleges. To my surprise, I received the same response from each school: *We don't take anyone who's divorced.* I even had a couple of schools tell me directly that God couldn't use me."

My initial thought was, *Wow, that seems harsh.* I tried to imagine receiving such a negative response; it had to be so discouraging. Even so, Ginger didn't give up. She was determined to learn more about God and serve Him, and she finally found a tiny college in Wyoming that accepted her application—with the stipulation that she could not date. Ginger was fine with that restriction and eager to start her classes. Unfortunately, her excitement was short lived.

"As soon as I arrived, it was apparent I was 'different' from everyone else, and they all knew it. It was not a friendly environment; lots of critical people." Once again she was told that God couldn't use her, this time by professors. "That hurt so much," she said.

I could tell, because I could still hear the hurt in Ginger's voice and I noticed her posture stiffen as she started talking about her experience there.

She continued, "I remember calling home and just crying and crying, and my dad telling me to come home. But I was learning a lot and felt like God was calling me to be a missionary. Plus, there were a few people who were supportive and encouraged me. So I stuck it out for the year, but it was absolutely hell the whole nine months I was there."

The following year Ginger transferred to a different Christian college. They had the same no-dating rule because she was divorced, but after observing her actions for about six months, the restriction was removed.

"My senior year I started dating a guy, and the relationship became serious," Ginger told me. "He knew I was divorced, and it wasn't a problem with him. But about a month before graduation, his parents found out I was divorced, and they freaked out. So he took me out to dinner, bought me roses, and told me, 'I have to break it off with you because my parents don't approve.' I was absolutely, positively crushed. We had planned on going into ministry together."

I tried to put myself in Ginger's shoes. I would have felt shocked, dumbfounded, embarrassed. But the longer I thought about it, words like *offended*, *hurt*, and *angry* surfaced.

Ginger must have gone through a similar progression of emotions. She continued, "Like I said, I was crushed. I kept thinking about what had happened. I dwelled on it and be came bitter and angry—absolutely totally angry, mostly at Christians."

It wasn't a surprise to hear that after she graduated, Ginger didn't go to the mission field. Instead, she moved back home—with a bad attitude, she said. "I was still mad and sick and tired of judgmental Christians."

FIGHTING AGAINST GOD

I understood why Ginger said she had been angry with Christians, but I couldn't help but think, *Maybe so, but you're actually angry with God.* There's no winning if we choose to go against God's ways, and Ginger was about to experience that firsthand.

> THERE'S NO WINNING IF WE CHOOSE TO GO AGAINST GOD'S WAYS.

"Next thing you know, I meet this guy," Ginger said. "He was a good ol' boy, you know. Liked to party and have fun. He was divorced, too, and I thought, *Well, I'll just go out with him. He certainly won't care if I'm divorced.*"

You know that feeling when you're sitting in a movie and can sense that something bad is going to happen? Well, that's what came over me as Ginger started telling me about dating this guy.

She continued, "Things got serious. I knew with all my heart, soul, and mind—everything within my being—it was wrong, totally wrong. But the hurt and my anger toward

Christians was controlling me. I started going to the bars with Tim, all the while getting further and further away from God. I knew I was sinning but didn't stop. In fact, I moved in with Tim."

Like I said, a bad feeling. Ginger told me she even felt like she had looked God in the face and said, "Yes, I'm going to do this." Ginger was intentionally turning her back on God. But God didn't turn His back on her. Not too long after moving in with Tim, Ginger went to church one Sunday and felt deeply convicted.

As Ginger began to recall details, her delivery intensified and she sat forward in her chair, telling me, "So I ran away, back to my aunt and uncle's. I was miserable, feeling torn and guilty. Here I'd once been immersed in God's Word and living for the Lord, and now I'm living with some guy. Just guilt, guilt, guilt."

As Ginger was retelling her story, I couldn't help thinking, *This has to be a turning point; God has finally gotten Ginger's attention.* But I was wrong. Ginger ended up taking another step away from God, returning home when Tim called and promised marriage.

"My godly aunt tried to counsel me spiritually, but I wanted to be married and had already made up my mind that no Christian guy would want me."

Ginger continued, "Within a couple of weeks after returning, I felt a huge weight on my heart, like a million pounds—*this is wrong, this is wrong, this is wrong.* But I was more afraid of not getting married again than doing what was right. So I married him."

Only six weeks into the marriage Ginger was contemplating leaving. Tim was drinking all the time. He was going straight to the bar after work and staying there late into the evenings. The situation was bad, but as Ginger explained, it was about to get worse.

A NEW ADDITION

"Then we got a call from Tim's ex-wife saying Tim's eight-year-old son wanted to come live with us. I was shocked. I remember crying and Tim saying, 'I really would like to have my son. He's in a terrible, terrible situation.'"

Ginger told me that she and Tim felt like they couldn't say no. Two months later, Tim's son, Chad, had moved in, and as you might expect, it wasn't smooth sailing. Ginger had never been a mom, and now she had a hyperactive, undisciplined boy in the house.

"I thought it was the most horrible thing that could ever happen, to have this kid come and live with us in the middle of a horrible marriage relationship." At this point, Ginger's face and voice softened. "But Chad coming to live with us saved my life spiritually, and it also saved Tim's life, literally and spiritually."

I asked Ginger to explain. She was visibly emotional as she continued. "God knew what He was doing. From the moment Chad came to live with us, my life changed, because God used that responsibility of having a child to help me get my life right with Him. And Chad coming into our home played a huge part in eventually getting Tim to stop drinking and turn his life over to the Lord." Ginger then described some of the changes in her that took place after Chad arrived. She confided, "I made a commitment that I was going to stick with the marriage, mostly for the sake of Chad. Even though I didn't really know him, God immediately started giving me those maternal feelings and a love for him."

I MADE A COMMITMENT THAT I WAS GOING TO STICK WITH THE MARRIAGE.

Ginger then put her hand up to her heart and looked at me, saying, "He is my son, and I love him more than anything." I already knew that, but it was so sweet to experience that moment with her.

Chad's moving in ended up being a wonderful thing, but Ginger and Tim's marriage was extremely difficult for the next year and a half. She said, "When you live with an alcoholic, in a sense you become sicker than they are about control issues. Tim was a mess, but I was worse because somehow in my mind I thought, *If I could just make him see, if I could just make him feel guilty, if I could just make him 'x'*—you fill in the blank—*he would quit drinking.*"

In her efforts to control Tim and his drinking, Ginger tried tears, guilt, and manipulation, but nothing worked. Then she met a man who had lost his family because of alcoholism, and he convinced Ginger she should check out an Al-Anon group, a support group for family members of alcoholics.

A CHANGED APPROACH

Joining Al-Anon was the best thing for her, Ginger said. "The group talked about asking God to change *us*, instead of us trying to change anybody else. That was hard for me. But I was determined to try it."

I was curious about what Ginger actually did to implement this approach, so I asked her to give me an example. In large part it required her to quit trying to control and pressure Tim. "I had to start by thinking, *You want to go to the bar and drink your guts out tonight? Have a good time. It's not my responsibility.*

"Chad and I would go to church, and when we left, I wouldn't say, 'Tim, would you come? Chad's going to be in church without his father.' Instead, I'd say to Chad, 'Come on, we have to leave in twenty minutes to go to church.' I wouldn't even invite Tim to go. I left him alone.

"Sometimes Tim would respond by getting up and going to church, and other times he wouldn't. But little by little, he did start going to church more. He even began participating in church game nights, bowling get-togethers, and potluck meals." Ginger paused, and then smiled, saying, "The church people treated Tim so nicely."

It struck me how Tim's experience was the total opposite of Ginger's experience with Christians as a young divorcée. These people embraced Tim. Then Ginger began talking about the role her dad and mom played in Tim's salvation. It was obvious how much Ginger loved her parents and that she was grateful for how they treated her and Tim.

"My dad and mom were especially supportive and sweet with Tim. They loved him and accepted everything about him, never once saying, 'Did you go drinking last night?' Even when they saw him drunk a few times, they were never condemning."

God was working in Tim's heart, and the day came when he decided to turn his life over to Christ. Not long after this, Tim and Ginger moved to Kansas for Tim's job. They found a good church, Tim started growing spiritually, Ginger continued to grow, and their marriage grew stronger and stronger as a result.

Remember how this chapter began, with Tim and Ginger moving to Africa as missionaries? That was all part of God's plan. Ginger told me, "God is absolutely amazing, because almost twenty years to the day after I first committed to be a missionary and then turned my back on God, God called Tim and me to the mission field. I'm a firm believer that with God, all things are possible."

LISTENING TO GOD

Shortly after Chad moved in with them, Ginger made the commitment to start getting back into God's Word. The decision was a lifesaver, she said. God's Word became her anchor through extremely stressful times.

These days, Ginger enjoys what she calls devotional journaling, an approach she's used for many years to engage God's Word. There are basically three components to Ginger's journaling process.

"First I read a passage or chapter, noting it in my journal," she said. "Then I record information that stands out, pieces of Scripture that might lead to spending time looking up other things that have come into my mind from that passage."

So, component number one is reading and noting key aspects from a section of Scripture. Ginger told me she then likes to write out her thoughts and details about her day (component two). "It's kind of like I'm writing out a conversation with God. So I might write something like, 'Yesterday was such a bad day at work. I had that big conflict with those two teachers, and, God, I really need wisdom. I don't know what I'm going to do.'"

I loved hearing how Ginger makes her time so personal with God. The third component to Ginger's engagement in the Word involves prayer. "The last thing I do when I'm done considering a Scripture is to write out prayer requests and then pray for them. It's amazing to go back and see the tons of prayers that I ask, ask, ask, and God has answered."

GOD'S WORD BECAME HER ANCHOR THROUGH EXTREMELY STRESSFUL TIMES.

Now it was my turn to ask—to ask Ginger to describe her daily routine.

"I love just reading through the Bible," she said. "I don't follow a reading plan, because that can make me feel rushed. I enjoy spending time thinking through and considering passages. Sometimes I'll read the same Scripture for a week or more."

Ginger sat up and looked at me pretty excited. "In fact, I spent three months in Matthew 25 on the parable of the talents," she said. (Hearing that, I couldn't help but think, *Three months?*) "But I kept coming back because God was showing me so much out of those few verses.

"I have to read first thing in the morning. That's when I'm sharp. If I wait until later, my brain is dead. So I get up, take my shower, go out to the kitchen to get my cup of coffee, and then I head to my devotion place."

I've been in Ginger's home many times and knew exactly what space she was referring to. You really can't miss it if you're in her house. It's a big overstuffed chair in her living room with an end table and lamp next to it. And laying on that end table at all times is Ginger's Bible, a notepad and a pen, and sometimes a ruler or a marker.

Ginger continued, "I have to be alone and turn everything off because Satan is a master distractor. He can use things I love, like my husband or even my dog, to keep me from hearing God speak to me through His Word.

"Ephesians is my favorite book," she said, "because not only did God give me a second chance, after I was an idiot and blew it, He gave me a third chance. And then I did something stupid and married an unsaved man, and He gave me a fourth chance. So for me the single most important word is *grace*. God's grace has touched my heart and my life the most. And Ephesians is all about grace."

I was touched by her explanation: "I have a friend who says we're swimming in grace, and I love that picture. Ephesians 1:7-8 tells us, 'In him we have redemption through his blood, the forgiveness of our trespasses, according to the riches of his grace, which he lavished upon us, in all wisdom and insight . . .' I knew the day I married Tim that it was the biggest mistake in my life, but I did it anyway. So what did God do when I turned back to Him again? He showed grace. I love Ephesians because of that."

WHAT WE CAN LEARN FROM GINGER'S STORY

+ **God is all about second, third, fourth . . . chances.** God loves us, and although we may turn from God, He will not turn His back on us. God is in the business of restoration. He desires for us to be in relationship with Him.

+ **No one is too much of a sinner or too far gone to be saved.** Tim is a good example of this. For years, his life was partying, bars, and drinking. No one would have ever guessed that Tim would turn his life over to Christ and become a missionary. So often our tendency is to give up on people, to write them off where salvation is concerned. God doesn't write anyone off. His offer of salvation is for all, and as a follower of Christ, it's our job to tell others about God's love for them and salvation through Jesus Christ. So who do you know that isn't saved? And when can you introduce him or her to Jesus?

+ **Satan loves to derail Christians.** Even after we receive Christ as Savior, Satan wants to pull us off-track by hitting us at our weak points. This means that when we're stressed, angry, hurting, or feeling abandoned or rejected, we have to be careful not to allow Satan to come in and lead us down a bad path. We saw this clearly with Ginger. Her initial shock and anger in response to condemnation and a broken relationship turned to bitterness and resentment and ultimately resulted in a total turning away from God.

+ **God can use you—regardless of your background.** If you've ever felt like you aren't good enough for God or that you can't serve Him because of "x" (you fill in the blank), think again. Satan loves to sell us the lie that we can't serve God, and for some reason, we buy into it. God created us to serve Him, and your unique background—even a horrible one—can be the exact thing that God will use to reach people in your neighborhood, on an airplane, at your church, in your workplace, at your hair salon.

+ **Our worst can be used for God's good.** For Ginger, Tim's son coming to live with her and Tim seemed like the worst possible situation. Instead, it got Ginger back on track with God and softened Tim's heart to hear the Holy Spirit. Ginger told me, "Without Chad coming, I'm not sure where we would be today. At the time I thought it was a really bad thing, but in reality, Chad becoming part of our married life was the best thing to ever happen."

So, is there something in your life now, or in your past, that seems terrible? Ask God how you might use that experience—to grow closer to Him, to help someone else going through a similar situation, to draw others to Christ by sharing your story.

RESPONDING TO GOD'S WORD

As Ginger revealed, her favorite book of the Bible is Ephesians, and her preferred way to engage God's Word is to spend focused time on a particular passage for several days. So we're going to follow in Ginger's footsteps. Here's a weeklong plan I tried; something I'd suggest for you, too.

Day one, read the entire book of Ephesians. (Ephesians is six chapters long, so if this is too much for one day's reading, break it into two days.) As you read, ask God to show you a specific passage to consider deeply the rest of the week.

Then, on each following day, read only your selected passage and ask God which specific elements He wants you to focus on. Write down what He is showing you and responses that come to your mind, including questions or prayers—whatever God lays on your heart. When you come back to that passage the next day, follow the same routine again. At the end of the week, look back over what God has revealed and taught you. At this point you can choose to stay on that passage longer or move on to another.

The following is my experience when I tried this method of engaging God's Word while reading a section of Ephesians. You'll notice that I didn't move systematically through the chosen section. Each day the Lord directed my focus to different verses.

TAMI'S WEEK IN EPHESIANS

Day 1: Ephesians is a rich book, and one that I'm quite familiar with. So I decided before I started to read that I wanted to focus on a passage that I hadn't necessarily given much attention to in the past. I asked God to show me what that passage should be, and when I began reading chapter 4 of Ephesians, I started feeling like the first half of that chapter was going to be my focused passage. Even so, I continued reading to the end of the book just to be certain. In the end, I decided Ephesians 4:1–16 would be my selected passage.

Day 2: With my spiral notebook and pen on the table in front of me, I prayed and asked God to show me something new from Ephesians 4:1–16. (I did this as part of my starting routine every day.) I then read the passage. In the very first verse, the phrase "walk in a manner worthy of the calling to which you have been called" caught my attention. I considered this phrase piece by piece. Here's what I wrote in my notebook:

Ephesians 4:1-16 (verse 1)

* *"called to serve"—I am called to share Christ.*

* *"walk worthy"—what does that mean? It means I need to watch my speech, my attitude, how I*

respond to people and circumstances. I need to be spending time in God's Word and being an active part of the body of Christ.

* "walk"—This lets me know I should be growing and moving forward spiritually. I can _only_ do this when I'm intentional in my Bible reading and prayer.

Day 3: Ephesians 4:1-16 (verses 4-6):

* Shows completeness of God.

* Shows that we are to work together and function as a body. I see this clearly from Paul's use of "One" seven times; "One" used seven times in three verses.

* Shows that all paths or religions _do not_ lead to salvation. Very absolute. Paul leaves no doubt that God is in control, and we serve Him.

* Shows that God isn't hit or miss.

* Shows God is trustworthy.

* Shows God is sure, solid, and reliable.

Day 4: Ephesians 4:1-16 (verses 7-10)
Paul doesn't provide specifics about salvation in these verses (e.g., Christ coming to live among us, live perfect sinless life, die in our place and

rise from the dead, return to heaven), because he's talking to believers who already <u>know</u> Christ.

"Gift" means given.

Grace given to <u>each of us</u>, reinforcing it's a personal, individual decision.

Logic/reasoning displayed by Paul—"ascended" lets us know Christ also had to descend.

Day 5: Ephesians 4:1-16 (verse 2)

Verse 2 describes for us <u>how</u> to walk in a worthy manner—"with <u>all</u> humility and gentleness, with patience, bearing with one another in love . . ."

Have I displayed this in the past week? Yes and no. I can do good one moment, and then a few minutes later respond poorly. This is a constant challenge.

These verses tell me that walking in a worthy manner requires me to be thinking about my walk, because if I just go about my day, I will stumble. Helps—prayer throughout my day (little prayers), Scripture reminders, listening to Christian music.

Day 6: Ephesians 4:1-16 (verses 11-16)

Big message I see: God expects us to grow spiritually.

There is more to our spiritual life than just salvation.

Verse 12—expects us to "work" for Him.

Verse 11—Gave us teachers and pastors to build us up. Shows that we aren't meant to operate alone, single-handedly.

When we are new believers or not yet spiritually

*mature, we are more susceptible to false teaching/
deceit because we don't yet <u>know</u> God's truth.*

Day 7: *Ephesians 4:1-16 (verse 1)*

*"I therefore, a <u>prisoner</u> for the Lord." Would I, could
I, be a prisoner for God? Yes, I'm sure I would be,
but I don't welcome that thought. I'm thankful for
the country I live in. Reminder of how we overlook
and take for granted the freedom we have to worship openly here. That being the case, why don't I
tell others more boldly? I could lose my life in some
places just for following Christ. We never know when
those freedoms may be taken away, and seems like
we are headed in that direction, incrementally.*

*<u>The National Anthem</u> is meaningful to me. I al-
ways sing it when I attend an event, and I always
tell God "thank you" in response to the song.*

*<u>Prayer: Thank you God, for how you have provid-
ed freedom for us to worship You. Help me take full
advantage of this freedom and be bolder to proclaim
and demonstrate You.</u>*

POST-EPHESIANS THOUGHTS

My experience focusing on Ephesians 4:1–16 was a good one.
I wasn't a stranger to this approach; I had already used it from
time to time. I definitely learn much more than my typical approach of reading a different Scripture passage each day. As I

continued to re-read the same passage day after day, I felt like I was uncovering the layers of what Paul was trying to convey. The repetition also reinforced the Scripture in my mind, as well as what I had already considered and recorded my prior times through the passage.

One big benefit of this assignment was that it made me slow down. I'm a type A person, so I can start pushing through Scripture quickly for the sake of finishing a chapter or book because I want to feel like I've accomplished something. That's a mistake. Yes, I'm still taking in God's Word and learning, but I know it results in far less than what God has for me. This assignment served as a reminder that I need to allow myself time to read and consider Scripture. The second day into this exercise, I thought to myself, *I could literally spend a month on this passage, no problem.*

Again, I encourage you to spend focused time in Ephesians. If you enjoy it, keep reading it for a while. Spending focused, quality time in God's Word is a wonderful way to get to know God better. And when you come across a verse, passage, chapter, or book that is speaking to you, ask God to show you what He wants you to learn, and then stay there until you believe it's time to move on.

CHAPTER 4

A LIFE RESTORED:

JEANNIE'S STORY

"I remember waking up from the anesthesia, laying on my bed and reciting the Lord's Prayer . . . I got dismissed from the clinic, and my mom and I headed back to the bus station. I was cramping and discharging all the way, which made for a long bus ride home. My dad was waiting for us. When we got into his pickup, he didn't say a word, but I could tell what he was thinking—You're putting me out. You've ruined your life. You've shamed our name. Feeling utterly rejected, my only thought was, Okay, I'm just going to take it one day at a time, and nobody's going to hurt me again."

THE FIRST TIME I talked with Jeannie, she seemed very soft spoken and mild mannered. I was actually worried that I may have scared her a bit, because I'm such an extrovert. Apparently I didn't overwhelm her, because today we are friends.

Jeannie is a mom to three grown kids, two girls and a boy, and also a grandma. From our early talks, it didn't take long to sense her passion for helping people and telling them about God's love and forgiveness. And she actively lives out that passion, working at her local crisis pregnancy center and co-leading women's Bible studies at her church. I like that about Jeannie.

So when I heard her life story, I was shocked because the Jeannie I knew seemed so different from the person she was in her younger years. God has truly transformed Jeannie.

JEANNIE'S STORY

Jeannie grew up in a family of six—Dad, Mom, and four kids. Her parents were not church-goers. In fact, her dad was very much anti-church. The environment in their home was tense. "I remember a lot of fear growing up," Jeannie told me. "We operated in a state of personal anxiety. It was a struggle, because you never knew what would set my dad off."

Without a stable home environment, Jeannie spent a lot of her afterschool hours at friends' homes. Jeannie recalled, "I didn't want any friends to come to my house, because I didn't know if my dad would be volatile or not."

"Was your dad's anger verbal or physical?" I asked.

"My dad was very verbal, very condescending," Jeannie responded. "There was a lot of 'You just don't measure up.'"

Jeannie desperately wanted her dad's approval but didn't know how to get it. Her dad was very strict, and there seemed to be no pleasing him. By the time she reached high school, Jeannie had given up on having a relationship with her dad, and became very rebellious.

"I defied my parent's authority. I was acting out sexually, staying out beyond my curfew. My attitude was, *I've tried to please you, but I never will, so I'll just do my thing.* And I did."

Not surprisingly, Jeannie left home as soon as she had the opportunity. At nineteen she moved to Norfolk, Virginia, to live with her brother and his wife. It was not a smart move for Jeannie. She now had total freedom and didn't know how to handle herself.

"I was a woman of the world," she said sarcastically. "I was going to the bars and in party mode. My brother tried to warn me, telling me that I was too young and had no idea what I was doing. But I wouldn't listen. I was in escape mode."

SURE ENOUGH, HER RECKLESS BEHAVIOR CAUGHT UP WITH HER.

Jeannie would have been wise to listen to her brother because, sure enough, her reckless behavior caught up with her. After one of her nights of partying, she had a one-night stand and got pregnant. Panic-stricken, she tried to push the situation out of her mind. "I didn't want to believe it could be a possibility," she told me. "I'd been promiscuous since I was fourteen and had escaped getting pregnant so many times before."

Rather than coming clean, Jeannie called home and told her parents she wanted to come home because she was homesick. Her rationale for not telling the truth was that she hadn't confirmed her pregnancy through a pregnancy test.

When Jeannie got home, however, she came to her senses and told her mom she thought she was pregnant. "It broke her heart," Jeannie said. The pregnancy was confirmed, and then Jeannie had to decide what to do next. "I wanted to move out, but I knew I couldn't manage things on my meager salary, and I didn't have any friends to share an apartment with, either. So my mom and I told my dad."

Fear, shame, regret, and *helplessness* are just a few of the words that flooded my mind as I imagined how Jeannie felt at that moment. It had to be awful.

"The reaction from my dad was not surprising," she told me. "He called me terrible names, and then proceeded to say he would not have a bastard child in his home. That crushed me."

That conversation took place years ago, but even so, Jeannie's voice betrayed the hurt she still felt from her dad's angry, foul response.

"I so wanted to please him. My telling him I was pregnant was probably like taking a sharp knife and sticking it in his heart. We lived in a town of four hundred, so everybody knows your business. And then, the abortion word came up."

Jeannie didn't know what to do and had nowhere to turn. She shut down emotionally, mentally, and physically, so her mom took the reins and put a plan together for Jeannie to go to Kansas for an abortion. Jeannie got a $500 loan under false pretenses, and as soon as she had cashed her paycheck, she and her mom were on a bus headed for Kansas.

Jeannie told me what little she remembers from that day. "I was under general anesthetic, which, as I look back, was a blessing. The abortion was performed in a very sterile environment in a hospital setting. I remember waking up from the anesthesia, laying on my bed, and reciting the Lord's Prayer."

The Lord's Prayer detail surprised me, because Jeannie had told me that church wasn't a part of her upbringing. "Where did that come from?" I asked.

"I don't know. I knew I'd done something serious. But I know now that God placed that in my mind. I knew the prayer from a Vacation Bible School I had attended. But that's about all the biblical instruction I'd had."

My heart was breaking for the Jeannie of time long past. That Jeannie was a mess, emotionally and physically. And to make matters worse, she had little support. She didn't have any real spiritual knowledge or foundation to draw on either.

A few hours after the abortion, Jeannie and her mom were on their way back home. "I got dismissed from the clinic, and my mom and I headed back to the bus station," Jeannie told me. "I was cramping and discharging all the way, which made for a long bus ride home. My dad was waiting for us. When we got into his pickup, he didn't say a word, but I could tell what he was thinking—*You're putting me out. You've ruined your life. You've shamed our name.* Feeling utterly rejected, my only thought was, *Okay, I'm just going to take it one day at a time, and nobody's going to hurt me again.*"

> JEANNIE WAS IN A DOWNWARD SPIRAL WITH ONE BAD DECISION LEADING TO ANOTHER.

After the abortion, there was no further discussion about it, and Jeannie went back to work like nothing ever happened. She started dating her brother's best friend, Rod. He was a nice guy, and Jeannie's dad really liked him. Rod became almost like a second son to her father.

Jeannie was still longing for that father-daughter relationship, and saw Rod as a way to get it. "I decided this was one way to get my dad's approval. I was going to marry this guy. But first he had to ask me. And he did."

Jeannie continued, "So it's two months after the abortion, and we're engaged, but I was dating other guys in-between."

I must have looked surprised, because Jeannie said sarcastically, "No grass grows under my feet." She hesitated for a moment and then went on. "I was living with my parents and acting out, staying out all night, doing stupid stuff. I had an engagement ring on my hand, but I was still seeing guys. And then I got pregnant again."

Making the matter even worse, the baby was not Rod's. And at this point I was wondering what in the world Jeannie was going to do. From my perspective, there wasn't any good ending in sight.

Jeannie did not want to abort the baby and was panicked. Rod would know he wasn't the father, because they hadn't slept together. "So we moved the wedding date up," Jeannie said, "and then I made sure Rod and I had sex. I seduced him, because I was going to make it appear that this baby was his."

Oh, the tangled web we weave immediately popped into my mind. Jeannie was in a downward spiral with one bad decision leading to another. She ended up miscarrying the baby in her upstairs bedroom by herself. "It was horrible," she said. "I didn't tell anyone. As far as I was concerned, this was another secret that was going to my grave with me." Jeannie paused for a moment, and then added, "So Rod and I had a lovely wedding from all appearances, but it was not the wedding of my dreams because my heart was not there."

"Where *was* your heart at this point?" I asked.

"It was pretty much shut down. I wasn't feeling anything. I wanted to move on with my life. My thinking was, *I'm married, and everything is going to be just so much better.* That was my dream—to erase the past."

That dream life didn't become reality, at least not for a while. Problems cropped up quickly, with money being a big one. Jeannie and Rod lived in a little town where Rod was a teacher. Jeannie wasn't working and wanted to have a baby. Rod wanted to wait, but Jeannie refused to let it go until Rod gave in. Jeannie described her actions this way: "What Jeannie wanted, Jeannie got, mostly by making everyone else miserable until they gave in."

Jeannie's pregnancy went smoothly, and she and Rod had a healthy nine-pound baby boy the first year they were married. Chip was the light of Jeannie's life. "I didn't realize that he was a gift from God," Jeannie told me, "but I had this sense that I was okay now with God because He had given me a child."

I didn't quite understand Jeannie's thinking. "What do you mean by 'okay with God'?" That's when Jeannie shared with me that during her pregnancy she was very fearful that God might punish her or punish her baby. She had actually had a nightmare when she was seven months along and cried out, "God, please don't hurt my baby!" Rod heard Jeannie's words, and that led Jeannie to tell Rod about her abortion.

"As I told Rod that I had gotten pregnant and aborted my child, I was grieving and bawling. I expected him to reject me, but he absolutely did not. Instead, he held me and comforted me. It was clear that he loved me and wanted to be married to me."

Even with Rod's loving response, Jeannie continued to struggle with her past and feelings of guilt. In her mind, she could not accept a free pass. "I knew in my heart that I needed judgment, I needed punishment. So I spent the next twenty-five years on a self-destructive road, and in the process I hurt my husband and family in untold ways."

Sometime after Jeannie opened up about the abortion, when she and Rod were no longer living near Jeannie's family, one of Rod's co-workers, a Mormon, invited Rod and Jeannie to church. Even though Jeannie hadn't been raised in church, she decided that little Chip needed to be there. So they went and Jeannie liked it. Family and community were important, and this drew Jeannie in. Rod didn't really care for it, but he went along with Jeannie for the sake of their marriage.

"I knew our marriage was on life support, but the Mormon Church infused me. Rod was willing to do whatever it took to help me feel okay. And I was feeling okay. I felt empowered as a woman and as a mother."

For the next thirteen years, Jeannie and Rod were members of the Mormon Church, and during that time they had two daughters. Still, Jeannie continued to battle the lingering fear that one of her children would die. "I didn't realize it at the time, but because I didn't have a relationship with God and I had basically no knowledge of the Bible, I had no real refuge or safety net. I was emotionally and spiritually bankrupt."

Then, when a young friend of Jeannie's daughter was killed in an accident, Jeannie's fear got the best of her. She demanded the family move back to their hometown, and Rod complied. The move, however, didn't resolve Jeannie's issues or their worsening marital problems. At this point, Jeannie was considering divorce. She and Rod had been married twenty-two years, and she wanted out, because, as she told me, "I'd been living a lie and I was sick of my life."

Jeannie wanted Rod to initiate the divorce, but he wouldn't. They did, however, end up separating. With Chip in college at this point, Rod took the girls and stayed in the community where he was teaching and Jeannie moved home with her widowed mom.

The separation didn't do a thing to change Jeannie's selfish heart or dissipate her anger. "I was horrible to Rod during this time," she said. "I really dogged him badly to my mom, trying to twist her mind against him. It was ugly, ugly, ugly. As much as I hated my father and didn't ever want to be like him, I was turning into him. I was replicating that horrific, angry minefield in my family."

Quite a ways into the separation, Rod called and made arrangements for him and the girls to take Jeannie to a movie. It was right after Christmas, and the temperature was well below zero. Rod had an old beater of a car, and when he didn't arrive on time, Jeannie's fears about losing a child took over. She was frantic. In this terrible state of mind, Jeannie headed out to try to find Rod. When she didn't find them, she called home only to discover that Rod and the girls had arrived. Jeannie blew up and drove back furious.

When Jeannie got back to her mom's, she unloaded big time on Rod. She recalled, "Rod met me at the back door. He tried to embrace me, but I physically pushed him away and told him to go back to the bedroom so we could talk. Once we got there I unleashed on him vile words, venom, and hatred for twenty minutes. And like he'd done so many times, he sat there and took it."

The picture I had in my head was a spoiled child throwing a tantrum—only this child was a full-grown adult named Jeannie.

Jeannie continued, "I told Rod, 'I'm done with this marriage. I'm done pretending. I've never loved you, because it was a joke.'"

As Jeannie turned to leave the room she expected Rod to let her go, but she got a surprise. Rod got up, shut the door, and then moved to within a few inches of Jeannie's face. "With his eyes locked on mine, Rod told me, 'Jeannie, I love you and I'm going to fight for this marriage. You can walk if you want to walk. But first you're going to tell the kids why you're leaving. You're going to own up to everything you've done, because I'm not going to be the bad guy here.'"

As you can imagine, Jeannie didn't know quite what to do or how to respond. For once she was speechless. "I had tried all these times to get him to divorce me, so I would be the wounded one, the victim. But Rod had really turned the tables on me."

Jeannie wasn't willing to tell the kids what she'd done and the horrible ways she had behaved over the years. So she, Rod, and the girls went to the movie. As Jeannie put it, "It was twenty degrees below zero outside and it was twenty below in my heart—at least for that moment."

Jeannie had finally hit rock bottom. The events of the evening were awful, but they served to turn Jeannie's focus to where it had never been before—God.

A CHANGED HEART

"That night, I cried out to God," Jeannie said. "'Lord, I've done everything wrong. I've hurt You. I've hurt my husband. I've hurt my children. I can't do this anymore. I need you, God!' I don't know where that came from, but I'm convinced it was a gift from God—it was His remembering me. That's where God reached down into my spirit. That's where I was saved, in that very room."

Jeannie admitted, "I needed a tearing down in my life. In my mind's eye, I saw Jesus, competing for me, and I saw the pain I caused and knew it was time to tell the truth. In that breaking and rebuilding, He took my hard heart and transformed it." She paused briefly, and then added, "One of my favorite verses is Ezekiel 36:26—'And I will give you a new heart, and a new spirit I will put within you. And I will remove the heart of stone from your flesh and give you a heart of flesh.' That's exactly what God did for me."

As Jeannie recalled that pivotal time in her life, I was struck by the depth of God's love. God never turned His back on Jeannie, and He won't turn His back on us, either. He

ROD TOLD ME, 'JEANNIE, I LOVE YOU AND I'M GOING TO FIGHT FOR THIS MARRIAGE.'

was patiently waiting for her to turn and cry out to Him, and when she did, He welcomed her with open arms. And that low-point-turned-high-point started Jeannie down the road of reconciliation with her husband and family. She described it as a "reconstruction job" on both her and Rod.

"Rod and I were now spending precious time together without anger and rage. We were in the process of renewing our relationship and discovering true love. We both realized that this was nothing we'd done on our own; it was absolutely a work of God."

Jeannie stopped her story for a moment and gathered her thoughts. "As we moved forward we stumbled and failed over and over, but in a different way than before, because now we were committed to doing things God's way. And in this healing process, God was pouring love into my heart."

I was smiling, thankful for how God is all about restoration, and happy for Rod and Jeannie. About two months into their new relationship, Rod and Jeannie decided they needed to talk with their kids about what had happened between them and ask the kids for forgiveness. Although they didn't all understand it immediately, over time their family relationship was healed.

LISTENING TO GOD

At this point I wanted to know how Jeannie nurtured her relationship with God after she surrendered her life to Christ. She quickly told me, "Number one, I wanted to get into the Bible." Of course, hearing that brought a smile to my face.

"Okay, so where did you start? How did you begin?" I asked.

I could tell Jeannie was thinking back, recalling things. She told me, "After I told my mom, I called my grandma who'd been praying for us for years. I said, 'Grandma, I know God has done something in my heart. So where do I go from here?

What do I do?' She told me to read the book of Romans. So I dove into Romans, and I read and I read. I was so amazed at God's love."

A sweet look came over Jeannie's face as she continued. "Romans 8:1—'There is therefore now no condemnation for those who are in Christ Jesus'—just nailed it for me. I was no longer condemned."

The more Jeannie read her Bible, the more her relationship with God grew. She approached her reading like it was taking her on a journey, like it was an unwrapping of God's Word. And as she continued to take in more of God's Word, she began to see God's hand in everything.

I loved what Jeannie told me next.

"God guided us, He provided for us, and I was able to give my abortion to Him and know that I was no longer defined by that; I didn't have to walk in that grief. Before coming to Christ I lived on nothing but disgrace, shame, and guilt, all the time putting on this phony front that everything was okay. I don't have to live that way—nobody does with Christ."

> IN THIS HEALING PROCESS, GOD WAS POURING LOVE INTO MY HEART.

JEANNIE'S TIME IN THE WORD

I knew Jeannie's relationship with God had continued to grow over the years. She had mentioned some things such as keeping a small devotional in her purse and having a Scripture app on her tablet, but I wanted to know what her regular time with God looked like.

WHEN I QUIT SKIMMING THE SURFACE AND REALLY DUG INTO THE WORD, IT WAS LIFE-CHANGING.

"What are you doing consistently to engage God's Word today?"

Without hesitation, Jeannie responded, "I spend time with God in the evening. I have a desk, my own little nook, and nobody touches that nook. I have my Bible wide open, and it's an amazing Bible with lots of pictures in it. I'm visual, I have to see pictures. It gives a lot of history, background, and context. I enjoy looking for things like, What's the background story here? Why did they do this? What's the significance of this? This type of information helps keep me on track."

Writing is also an important part of Jeannie's time with God. "I read and then I write Scripture verses in my notebook," she said. "Under that I write my understanding of the verse and how it's impacting me. I also write observations of what God's Word is teaching me and what specifically is training my heart."

But Jeannie explained there is another reason for writing out Scripture. "I'm writing because I don't know what the future holds. But if I ever have my Bibles taken away from me,

I have this tablet with me full of Scripture and my thoughts."

Consistently spending time in God's Word is essential for our spiritual growth (see appendix). And that was certainly Jeannie's experience. When she finally got to a place of having a daily routine, it was life transforming.

Jeannie shared, "For a long time I would start and stop with my Bible reading. I'd start reading in Genesis and do all right until I hit Leviticus. Then maybe I'd just read out of the New Testament. It wasn't effective."

I could identify with Jeannie's experience, because I had once faced similar frustrations. Jeannie continued, "When I quit skimming the surface and really dug into the Word, it was life-changing. Marinating in God's Word has brought me a sense of calm and peace that was lacking before. God's Word has transformed me."

JEANNIE TODAY

Jeannie and Rod have been married more than forty years, and are going strong now that the Lord is at the center of their marriage. Today, Jeannie is making full use of her life story, working at her local crisis pregnancy center and speaking to women's groups. She is especially passionate about helping post-abortive women experience healing, both emotionally and spiritually, through a relationship with Jesus Christ.

WHAT WE CAN LEARN FROM JEANNIE'S STORY

+ **Words are powerful.** Words can build people up or tear them down. Harsh, critical, negative words can have a devastating impact. Jeannie's relationship with her dad provides a distinct picture of the emotional damage words can cause. We need to be mindful of every word that comes out of our mouths, with the goal of speaking the truth in love, and building others up rather than tearing them down.

+ **Satan loves to remind us of our failures and wrongs.** Satan wants to keep us from serving God, and one of his tactics is to remind us of our past failures and wrongs. As followers of Christ, we are forgiven! Jeannie's key verse, Romans 8:1, says it all: "There is therefore now no condemnation for those who are in Christ Jesus." Claim the promises of God's Word and don't give Satan one inch.

+ **God's forgiveness is bigger than our sin.** God is in the business of forgiving sin, and nothing you have done will make Him turn away from you. He is waiting and will welcome you with open arms. First John 1:9 tells us, "If we confess our sins, he is faithful and just to forgive us our sins and to cleanse us from *all* unrighteousness."

+ **God can use the most horrific events for His glory.** Sometimes it's necessary for us to go through a set of difficult circumstances or experience something terrible to bring us into relationship with God. That's what happened with Jeannie. The more her life spiraled out of control, the more she realized she needed God and surrendered her life to Him. That changed everything. Today, Jeannie is using her story to reach women with the message that Christ's love is for them. Romans 8:28 says, "And we know that for those who love God all things work together for good, for those who are called according to his purpose."

RESPONDING TO GOD'S WORD

The book of Romans is where Jeannie began her journey in God's Word and where she first understood God's love for her. Romans 8 was especially meaningful for her, so we're going to spend time in that chapter this week. And because writing out Scripture is a big part of Jeannie's routine, that will be our focus, as well.

We'll start each day reading a portion of Romans 8. Then, in a notebook we'll write out all the verses we just read. Mark any verse that is significant to you. Once that's done, look back over the passage and write down your observations. Questions you might consider asking yourself: What's my understanding of this passage and why? How did it impact me? What is this passage teaching me? As you read and write, make sure to note specifics, such as an example or a command you need to put into practice, or a word or phrase that really speaks to you. I'll go first, so you can see a little about how I engaged with my Day 6 reading, and then it's your turn. Have fun!

Here's how I broke down Romans 8 each day. You can follow this schedule, or read and write at whatever pace works best for you.

Day 1: Romans 8:1–4

Day 2: Romans 8:5–8

Day 3: Romans 8:9–11

Day 4: Romans 8:12–17

Day 5: Romans 8:18–25

Day 6: Romans 8:26–30

Day 7: Romans 8:31–39

Romans 8:26-30

26. Likewise the Spirit helps us in our weakness. For we do not know what to pray for as we ought, but the Spirit himself intercedes for us with groanings too deep for words.

27. And he who searches hearts knows what is the mind of the Spirit, because the Spirit intercedes for the saints according to the will of God.

28. And we know that for those who love God all things work together for good, for those who are called according to his purpose.

29. For those whom he foreknew he also predestined to be conformed to the image of his Son, in order that he might be the firstborn among many brothers.

30. And those whom he predestined he also called, and those whom he called he also justified, and those whom he justified he also glorified.

What I understood and took away from verses 26–27:

+ The Holy Spirit is my helper and advocate. He intervenes on my behalf with God.

+ I don't always know what's best for me or what is God's will, but the Holy Spirit does, and He is actively acting on my behalf.

+ It's comforting and reassuring to know that the Holy Spirit is residing in me and working on my behalf.

What I understood and took away from verse 28:

+ God is in control and has a master plan.

+ God is good, and His plan is for good.

+ The words "all things" let me know that every circumstance that arises or situation I go through is part of God's plan. Nothing that happens to me is a surprise to God.

+ This verse tells me *loudly* that I can trust God in every circumstance. Thank you, God!

What I understood and took away from verses 29–30:

+ I am called (I know Jesus). I am justified (righteous before God because of Jesus' death on the cross). I am glorified (I will spend eternity with God).

+ God wants me to be like Christ.

+ I am grateful for God's plan of salvation and His love for me.

+ Key phrases: "helps us in our weakness" and "all things work together for good."

POST-ROMANS 8 THOUGHTS

As I jumped into our Romans 8 assignment, it didn't take long to realize that writing out that day's verses required more discipline than simply reading, mainly because it takes more time. At first I thought that was a drawback, but actually it was a good thing for me because it made me slow down. Writing out the passages also caused me to focus more on the message, because I was only able to look at and consider three to four words at a time as I wrote. Little things like writing the word "Spirit" and using a capital "S" made me think about why I used that capital letter— because this is God. And, yes, I already knew that, but writing it out reinforced that nugget of information in my mind. If I had simply read the passage, I likely would have skimmed right over the word without thinking about it. So I definitely took more in from these four verses as a result of writing them out.

Overall, writing out Romans 8:26–30 was helpful for me. So would I choose to write out everything I read each day? Probably not everything, but will I continue to write out a key verse or maybe several verses from a particular passage from time to time? Absolutely.

All right, that's my experience. Now it's your turn to jump into Romans 8. And remember, like other times you engage God's Word, before you begin this "read and write" assignment, ask Him to show you something new every day through your writing.

Zoe started retelling her story

to me by bravely sharing

about her first marriage.

"After dating Cory for six years,

I married him at twenty-three.

We had a lot in common,

but the biggest thing was

that we were both Christians.

Neither of us ever dreamed

we'd get divorced. It was

'till death do us part.'"

CHAPTER 5

SPIRITUAL INTERRUPTIONS WELCOME:

ZOE'S STORY

*"I had the cancer kind of divorce. I did my crying and grieving
before we came apart, so that when we finally got to the point of divorce,
I was thinking, Please let me die, please let me out."*

SHARP, VIBRANT, confident, and professional was my immediate assessment of Zoe when I met her at a business conference several years ago. Although we live in different cities, Zoe and I developed a friendship over the next few years. And when we do get the chance to hang out together, it typically involves a coffee shop, because we both like a good cup of coffee.

As I've come to know Zoe, there's no doubt about it, she's a type A go-getter. She puts her high energy to good use, owning and managing a business. For several years she was a single working mom after getting divorced at a young age. Then she met and married Carson, who was also a divorced parent. When you're around Zoe and Carson, it's obvious they are best friends and enjoy spending time together, which is a good thing since they work together in Zoe's business.

ZOE'S STORY

Zoe started retelling her story to me by bravely sharing about her first marriage. "After dating Cory for six years, I married him at twenty-three. We had a lot in common, but the biggest thing was that we were both Christians. Neither of us ever dreamed we'd get divorced. It was 'till death do us part.'"

Zoe and Cory were a pretty typical couple. Both were career oriented, and as a result, they waited ten years before having any children. Unfortunately by ten years in, their marriage was unraveling.

Sipping on her cup of coffee, Zoe told me, "Looking back, I'd say we were the victims of what I call slow erosion."

"How so?" I asked.

She thought for a moment and then responded, "We weren't looking after foundational things like caring for our relation ship enough in terms of ultimate respect for each other, and putting God and His Word at the center of our marriage."

I assumed Zoe was going to tell me that going to church and taking in God's Word weren't an important part of their marriage. But that wasn't completely accurate. Church *was* very much a part of her and Cory's life, and they were going to Bible study groups, attending Christian conferences, and were even part of some leadership teams that put on marriage retreats. Yet something was keeping them from making God part of their daily thinking and decisions.

WERE WE OPERATING FROM A HEART LEVEL, ASKING GOD TO DIRECT THE DECISIONS WE WERE MAKING? I DON'T THINK SO.

Zoe told me point blank, "We weren't doing just the 'Sunday Christian' thing. We meant it when we were there. But were we operating from a heart level, asking God to direct the decisions we were making? I don't think so.

"As I look back, I don't recall loving prayer or loving Bible reading. I loved a good sermon or a good book written about Christian things, but I'm not sure the Bible was all that exciting for me. At that point, my Bible reading was only for the sake of Bible reading, rather than for the sake of changing me from within."

Zoe and Cory weren't seeking out the Lord or reading God's Word as a couple, either. It wasn't their norm to talk with God and to read about Him each day, so they weren't in tune to His guiding and directing. "There was little prayer together," she said. "There was on again, off again Bible reading. But God's Word wasn't permeating our hearts."

From all outward appearances, Zoe and Cory's marriage seemed fine. But their spiritual foundation, individually and as a couple, was weak. And behind closed doors, pornography and then infidelity were slowly tearing the marriage apart.

"I had the cancer kind of divorce. I did my crying and grieving before we came apart, so that when we finally got to the point of divorce, I was thinking, *Please let me die, please let me out.*"

Cory and Zoe decided to separate, which immediately thrust Zoe into a new and unfamiliar situation. She was now a single mom in her late thirties with a son who was two and a daughter who was five, and she didn't know what to do.

"It was horrible. During the first two years when we were separated but not yet divorced, I received letters from people telling me, 'Your God is too small.' A couple of people even sent me some case studies where there had been infidelity and the women had stuck by their husbands. And I'm thinking, *Well, isn't that marvelous?* So I struggled, asking myself things like, *Could I not be trusting enough? Am I doing the right thing?*"

Zoe and Cory tried to reconcile after they'd been separated about two years, but Cory showed little change of heart or change in actions. "It was one of the most difficult periods of my life," Zoe recalled. She tried for six months to work things out, "but we ended up divorcing, and then I truly joined a strange world of people."

That "strange world" comment certainly got my attention. With a little sigh, Zoe explained. "Cory and I had been really social and involved in our church. So we were invited to lots of things, went to lots of dinner parties, had lots of friends—as a couple. Now all of a sudden, I'm just Zoe, and Zoe by herself doesn't get invited to things. I know now that no one sat down and said, 'Oh, let's cross Zoe off the list,' but when they're inviting over the Jones and the Browns and the Smiths, single Zoe, or single Cory for that matter, doesn't fit in."

I totally got what Zoe was describing. In fact, I felt a little convicted, because I realized I had done the same thing as Zoe's friends many times. My husband and I would have a cookout or get-together, and I would shy away from inviting someone who was divorced and single, or just single, because it could be awkward. It wasn't because I didn't like the person; it was just easier that way. My heart went out to Zoe as she shared how isolated she felt.

"The awful thing is you don't feel any different. You're still a mom with kids, you still need friendship, you still want to be in mixed company. But you no longer fit into the rest of this church world. It's strange, because it's almost like you become a social outcast."

At this point Zoe leaned forward and said, "I've told people over the years that I should write a book titled *No Casseroles, No Flowers*, because I didn't get any flowers or casseroles or any offers to watch my children as I struggled through separation and divorce. Yet if something had happened to Cory, if he had had a bad accident or died, for example, I would have been the recipient of all those things."

Sadly, I had to admit she was right. I had a pretty good picture of the emotional side of Zoe. Now I wanted to learn how her divorce impacted her spiritually. The next thing I know, she was telling me about her tree.

TURNING OVER A NEW LEAF

"I don't remember exactly how it happened, but in this weird stage of singleness I realized I had to get and stay healthy in a number of areas," Zoe said. "So I thought of myself and came up with a picture of a tree with four roots growing down—a physical root, an emotional root, an intellectual root, and a spiritual root—and obviously the spiritual root is fundamental, absolutely fundamental."

I must have had an odd look on my face, because she explained, "The roots of a tree are what keep it alive, so I decided that I would feed each of those roots every single day. I felt that was the most balanced way I could move forward and be a healthy single mom." Back then, she even drew the tree, which she described as a "large, fat oak-like tree with great big, thick roots and all of these branches to represent the many different hats I wore."

She confided, "This exercise was kind of scary for me because, at the time, I was overwhelmed with my very, very busy life and trying to do so many things at one time. So when I drew the tree and branches, it helped me see that I wasn't going to have anything to get to those branches unless I fed my roots."

I liked Zoe's tree. It made sense to me. As she described her picture, I was actually thinking about what my tree might look like. And then one of my favorite Scripture passages came to mind.

> *Blessed is the man who walks not in the counsel of the wicked, nor stands in the way of sinners, nor sits in the seat of scoffers; but his delight is in the law of the Lord, and on his law he meditates day and night. He is like a tree planted by streams of water that yields its fruit in its season, and its leaf does not wither. In all that he does, he prospers.*
>
> —Psalm 1:1-3

I asked Zoe if her tree was the catalyst that got her engaged in God's Word regularly.

"Yes, it started as a discipline but ended up establishing patterns and a habit, which then turned into a habit fueled by a desire of the heart to be in God's Word. It was an important turning point for me.

"I can remember a couple nights, laying there in bed, mentally checking off my 'root list' and making myself get up because I'd neglected one of those roots. And sometimes it was the spiritual one."

I smiled hearing about Zoe's experience, because I have done the same thing a few times—gotten out of bed after just climbing in because I had neglected to read my Bible. I had to ask, "Was thinking of yourself as a tree the moment when you truly 'got it' that God's Word had to be your foundation?"

Zoe responded, "Most definitely, that's when I decided God needed to be a part of my everyday life and my everyday thinking. That's when something switched in terms of thinking of Bible reading or prayer as something I *had to do* to be a 'good girl.' Instead, they became things *I wanted to do* because now Jesus Christ was my best friend."

FEEDING THE TREE

I wanted to know what Zoe was doing to feed her spiritual root. She told me she used a variety of study guides to give her structure and direction, as well as a sort of subliminal accountability with regard to reading the next day's lesson. I liked what she told me next.

"I always read the passage from my own Bible, because I love writing what I see directly in my Bible. My Bible is literally loaded with things I've noted. I never want another Bible because everything is written in there."

Zoe then described what her study time looked like. "What I do is read the passage that's been outlined for the day and the comments. Then I'll read both again. I'm very application oriented, so as I'm reading, I'm always looking for and considering things like, *God, what do you want me to get from this today? What am I supposed to learn here? How am I supposed to apply it?*"

I was nodding my head and smiling because what Zoe described is Bible engagement—receiving God's Word, reflecting on it, and then responding to it. Zoe told me she typically spends no more than fifteen minutes on a particular reading, and the final part of that time is spent looking for a few key words to carry with her for the day.

"As I'm closing my Bible, I look for a few words—it might be a phrase from a verse or a truth that jumped off the page—that I'm going to say over and over throughout the day. For example, 'God will see you through this.' I might say that phrase a few times to myself, thinking, *That's the little gem I'm going to lock in my heart for the day.*"

So Zoe has a set, daily routine for studying God's Word that focuses her on God first thing in the morning. But she doesn't stop there. She also takes in Scripture throughout her day in smaller, bite-sized pieces via her cell phone and computer.

"I also love sound bites and short-feature Scripture helps throughout my day. This has actually become my favorite way of taking in God's Word over the past couple of years. I can really see how it has helped me grow spiritually."

Zoe continued, "Reading in general has always been a struggle for me. So audio pieces are easier for me to take in and understand. I look forward to receiving those touches from God's Word throughout my day."

> I ALSO LOVE SOUND BITES AND SHORT-FEATURE SCRIPTURE HELPS THROUGHOUT MY DAY.

I asked Zoe why she felt the daily multiple contacts with Scripture were so important and helpful. Her response was dead on, in my experience. "The many contacts help me refocus and stay in the present instead of thinking about things like past mistakes, hurts, or guilt."

To clarify, I asked, "So you're saying that taking in Scripture throughout the day counterbalances negative thoughts?"

"Yes," she replied, "and because I know that, I don't have any problem stopping what I'm doing for a couple of minutes to listen to an audio clip or read a short Scripture verse and comment. Looking back over the past year or so, I can definitely see there's been a cumulative effect. I can see a lot of growth spiritually as a result of many short encounters with God's Word."

goTandem

I loved everything Zoe had told me about bite-sized pieces of Scripture, because Back to the Bible has a ministry called *goTandem* that was created around short Scripture passages. *goTandem* uses mobile technology (cell phones, tablets) and the Internet to deliver short pieces of biblical content to people throughout their day. It's a 24/7 tool designed to encourage and nurture spiritual growth through daily Bible engagement, with content tailored to each specific recipient.

Zoe is a *goTandem* user, and she told me how much she enjoys it. "When you need a nugget of God's truth at various moments during the day, this is a great way to plug into the Word. It is easy and accessible, and it's designed to bring the Bible into my day, regardless of what is going on for me."

I'm a *goTandem* user, too, and totally agree with Zoe's response. What I appreciate most about *goTandem* is that you can get multiple messages each day, and you choose when you receive each one. So let's say 10:00 in the morning is a diffi cult time of the day, because you have a standing appointment with a grumpy person, or maybe that's when you're tempted to mentally check out of work and look at Facebook. Well, you can schedule a "spiritual interruption" from *goTandem* at that time each day to help you refocus on God and keep you on track until the next message comes, again, at a time of your choosing.

Zoe added, "While I like to think that I will pick up my Bible several times a day to read a verse or passage, it probably won't happen. I know there are a lot of people like me who could benefit from receiving inspirational interruptions throughout their day through *goTandem*."

Zoe and I had been talking for a couple of hours at this point, so as we finished our now cold coffee, I asked, "Is there a particular book of the Bible, or maybe a chapter or a verse, that was a buoy or a life support for you?"

She thought for a moment and then answered, "Proverbs 3:5—'Trust in the Lord with all your heart, and do not lean on your own understanding'—got me through lots. And then Philippians 4:7—'And the peace of God, which surpasses all understanding, will guard your hearts and your minds in Christ Jesus.' I still claim that a lot. One other verse that was so helpful was Jeremiah 29:11—'For I know the plans I have for you . . . plans for welfare and not for evil, to give you a future and a hope.' I actually didn't know that verse before my divorce. I might have heard it, but it didn't stand out. There were days when all I could say was, 'Okay, I'm just going to claim that there's hope.'"

ZOE NOW

After being a single mom for six years, Zoe met and then married Carson, who was also divorced and had two children. Zoe told me she felt blessed with this second chance, and that being a blended family is working well. She is thankful for a husband who is the spiritual leader of their home and for twelve years of marriage with God at the center.

Now that Zoe is on the other side of divorce, her heart is to help divorced people. "I try to come alongside and encourage and care for people in the church who are divorced, especially women."

WHAT WE CAN LEARN FROM ZOE'S STORY

+ **God has to be the center.** As a Christ-follower, God must be the focus and center of our life. And if we're married, God needs to be the foundation and center of the marital relationship as well. We saw that clearly through Zoe's story. Although Zoe and Cory were believers, they weren't fully focused on God individually. And in turn, God wasn't at the center of, or directing, their marriage. Zoe's description of her heart and those early years of marriage provides a good reminder of the importance of regularly assessing our focus and how we're doing spiritually, so we can take corrective action as needed.

+ **Attending church doesn't ensure spiritual maturity.** So often we lull ourselves into thinking that we're doing well spiritually because we've been at church every Sunday for the past six months, or because we're part of a small group, or we just attended a women's conference. But our "going" and how much we're "doing" aren't accurate measures of where we are spiritually. From all appearances, Zoe and Cory were doing the right things, but they were neglecting what was most important—seeking God through His Word. It's my hope that as you and I go through each chapter of *Off the Page & Into Your Life,* we'll grow spiritually as we seek God and engage His Word together.

+ **Divorce happens—even to Christians.** When two Christian people get married, the expectation is that the marriage will go well, because, after all, they're Christians. However, just because we're a Christ-follower doesn't mean our lives are going to be smooth sailing. In fact, the Bible tells us exactly the opposite, that we should expect hard times and difficult circumstances. That being the case, we need to be especially mindful of our marriage relationship.

+ **Being intentionally considerate should be a priority.** Zoe needed support in a number of ways when she became a single mom. But for whatever reason, most of the people around her weren't tuned in to that fact. Even worse, people treated her differently as a single person. There are plenty of "Zoes" in our lives. Let's use Zoe's story as a motivator to be intentional about looking around at church, at work, in our neighborhood, for people who are in need of support. Maybe they could use someone to talk to, they may be struggling financially, perhaps they have a physical limitation, or, like Zoe, maybe they need a babysitter from time to time. Would you take some time today and consider who it is you can help?

RESPONDING TO GOD'S WORD

Tree Drawing: A turning point in Zoe's life was her drawing a tree with four roots and numerous branches, which she then labeled. Being able to visualize all of her responsibilities on the top of the tree helped her realize even more the importance of sustaining her foundational roots, particularly the spiritual root. We're going to follow Zoe's lead and create our own tree. We'll do that at the end of the chapter where you'll find an outline of a tree for you to use. If it's too small, make a photocopy enlargement, or draw your own if you're feeling creative. You'll also find my completed tree diagram to get us started.

goTandem: The next step is to try *goTandem*. You can connect with *goTandem* by downloading the app or, if you don't have a smartphone, by signing up online at *goTandem.com*. It won't take long and it's easy. You'll answer a few questions to set up your profile, and you will also have the opportunity to take a short assessment that will tailor the content you receive specifically to you. Soon you will be receiving biblical content that speaks directly to the challenges you are facing.

goTandem offers several different types of content to help you receive, reflect on, and respond to God's Word. Here are a few examples to help you get a better understanding what you'll receive each day.

---

goTandem: Solid God

I know the Lord is always with me. (Psalm 16:8 NLT)

A needed reminder?

goTandem: A Clean Heart

Create in me a clean heart, O God.
Renew a loyal spirit within me. (Psalm 51:10 NLT)

What is the writer's desire in this verse? How would having a "loyal spirit" mold your thinking and decisions?

goTandem: Getting It All

Seek the Kingdom of God above all else, and
he will give you everything you need. (Luke 12:31 NLT)

What does it mean to seek God's kingdom?
What are some things you count on God for?

goTandem: Shedding Weight (audio)

All right: You are running—you're nearing the end of a footrace where the winner gets a years' supply of movie tickets and un-limited buttered popcorn refills. Oh, and the winner also gets a soda. You are close to winning, but, oh, someone throws a heavy jacket on you at the last second and then trips you with a broom handle. Bummer. No movie tickets for you.

The writer of Hebrews compares the Christian life to a race in chapter 12, verses 1-6:

> *Therefore, since we are surrounded by such a huge crowd of witnesses to the life of faith, let us strip off every weight that slows us down, especially the sin that so easily trips us up. And let us run with endurance the race God has set before us. We do this by keeping our eyes on Jesus, the champion who initiates and perfects our faith. Because of the joy awaiting him, he endured the cross, disregarding*

its shame. Now he is seated in the place of honor beside God's throne. Think of all the hostility he endured from sinful people; then you won't become weary and give up. After all, you have not yet given your lives in your struggle against sin. And have you forgotten the encouraging words God spoke to you as his children? He said, "My child, don't make light of the Lord's discipline, and don't give up when he corrects you. For the Lord disciplines those he loves, and he punishes each one he accepts as his child."

—Hebrews 12:6 (NLT)

So run! Run to win! Make Jesus your focus and you will endure!

goTandem: Fruitful Living: The Great Trade (audio)

Hi—*goTandem* here with a question for you about peace: Where does it come from, that inner calm, even when life's hard? See Romans 4:25-5:1 (NLT):

[Jesus] was handed over to die because of our sins, and he was raised to life to make us right with God. Therefore, since we have been made right in God's sight by faith, we have peace with God because of what Jesus Christ our Lord has done for us.

Peace can be a feeling, but it's way bigger than that. It's a fact. It's a gift. See, when we trust in God, we make this mind-boggling trade: we give Him our sin and chaos and God gives us His peace. This inner peace is the source of all peace in this world. And lots of people don't have it. But it's there, in you. Tap into it. And then tell someone who needs it.

TAMI'S TREE AND goTANDEM EXPERIENCE

The idea of displaying my life as a tree was fun to me. I was eager to see what it would look like so I jumped right in and labeled my roots, making sure that the spiritual root was the biggest one since it is by far the most important. That didn't take too long, and I didn't think labeling the branches with roles and responsibilities would take long either, but I was wrong. I underestimated the things I'm involved in and what I do from week to week. Altogether I spent about fifteen minutes completing my tree. I enjoyed the exercise because it made me realize that I am wearing quite a few hats. And, the visual aspect of it was helpful, as well, because it highlighted a few areas where I need to spend more time and a few where I could spend less. Here's my tree. (And remember, there's a blank tree diagram for you to use at the end of the chapter.)

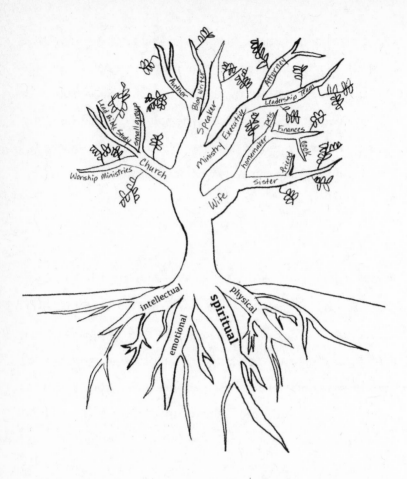

Since *goTandem* is part of the ministry of Back to the Bible, I have been a *goTandem* user for quite some time. There are a number of benefits to receiving *goTandem*. I like how it comes throughout the day at times and places where I wouldn't have a Bible with me. But because the messages are coming over my phone, short Scripture passages paired with application thoughts and questions are right in front of me. And when I read the *goTandem* messages, they immediately refocus me on God and get me thinking about what I've said that day, how I've acted, what I'm thinking, and how I can finish out the day. I've included an example of one of my *goTandem* messages below with my response underneath.

goTandem: Believe and Confess

If you confess with your mouth that Jesus is Lord and believe in your heart that God raised him from the dead, you will be saved. For it is by believing in your heart that you are made right with God, and it is by confessing with your mouth that you are saved.
—Romans 10:9–10 (NLT)

What is our hope from this verse? Is there something that stops you from sharing it with others?

My response: Our hope is salvation and spending eternity with God. How awesome is that? What stops me from sharing it with others varies. Sometimes I'm a chicken and don't say anything because I'm afraid someone won't like what I'm saying or won't like me. Other times I'm too busy or too focused on what I'm doing to even pay attention to opportunities to share Christ. And, I hate to admit it, there are times when I let myself think it's someone else's job, which is absolutely not true and lame on my part. I need to be an active and bold advocate for Christ—period.

POST-TREE AND *goTANDEM* THOUGHTS

I invite you to draw your own "tree" and try *goTandem*. The tree will help you focus on you and your spiritual needs and *goTandem* will help you grow spiritually. So I encourage you to get started today!

CHAPTER 6

LOVE OVERCOMES:

JULIE'S STORY

*"I totally felt like I was trash, no-good, bad, couldn't do anything right.
I didn't understand it or why I was doing the things I was doing . . .
I remember asking Jesus to please make me be a better person,
and thinking, Why am I doing these things that don't make sense,
when I want to serve You and love You?"*

JULIE IS A PASTOR'S WIFE, and has been heavily involved in church most of her married life. Her husband, Bob, is an outgoing people person. Have you ever heard the phrase "he knows no strangers"? That's Bob. As a couple, Bob and Julie are sweet. It's obvious they both love the Lord.

As I pulled up outside the church office where Julie and I had decided to meet, I looked up to see Julie waiting for me with her kind, sweet smile. Bob had arranged a nice quiet place for us to sit down and get comfortable. I had heard bits and pieces of Julie's story, but never the whole thing. So as we settled in, I was eager to learn more about Julie's life and experiences.

JULIE'S STORY

Julie was raised in a loving Christian family with one brother who is six years older than her. Her parents were hard working, but didn't have a lot of money. They built their own home little by little. Julie described it as living in a basement home for a few years until her parents saved enough money to allow them to add on a first floor.

Julie's parents came to Christ through a neighbor who invited them to church when Julie was very young. So Julie was basically brought up in church. "I remember when I was six that I wanted to be a Christian, too," she said. "I know that I didn't totally understand everything, but I believe that's when I gave my heart to Jesus. I've always had a real desire to serve Him."

After they were saved, Julie's parents still hung out with friends they had before giving their lives to Christ. But there was one couple, in particular, who came to Julie's home a lot, and that wasn't a good thing for Julie.

Julie was a pretty little girl, with long dark hair and green eyes. "By the time I was about three, when this couple would come over, the man would get me off somewhere and . . . you know."

I was pretty sure I knew what Julie meant, but I didn't want to assume anything, so I asked if the man had sexually abused her. "Yes," Julie said, "and I knew every time they came that he was going to do things to me. I remember wanting to hide when he would come over, and my parents would get after me because I wasn't being friendly."

Watching and listening to Julie talk about this horrific experience gave me a heavy heart, especially hearing that the abuse happened quite often because the two families got together frequently.

"As I recall, he told me not to tell anyone, and I didn't," she said. "I couldn't understand why my parents didn't see it and stop it. But I'm convinced they didn't know. I never did tell my parents, and now they're both with the Lord."

This family friend continued molesting Julie into her early teens. The repeated abuse affected Julie's thinking and behavior in ways she didn't understand, especially as she grew older. By the time Julie reached high school, she had become quite rebellious. Her parents were frustrated with her, and her self-esteem was almost non-existent.

I inwardly winced at Julie's next statements. "I totally felt like I was trash, no-good, bad, couldn't do anything right. I didn't understand it or why I was doing the things I was doing." Then she paused, adding, "I remember asking Jesus to please make me be a better person, and thinking, *Why am I doing these things that don't make sense, when I want to serve You and love You?*"

Julie told me that toward the end of high school, she became sexually active. "I'd sneak out at night. It was a bad scene. I never got into drugs or alcohol, but I was seeking something in the opposite sex."

With high school being such a rough time for Julie, when she changed her mind after graduation to attend a Christian college instead of nursing school, Julie's parents were all for it. "My parents jumped all over my going to Bryan College, because it was an evangelical Christian environment and the school had a strong focus on God and His Word. I was excited about it, too, and felt like God was telling me to go there. I thought, *This has got to be my answer. I've been asking Jesus to get me out of my situation.* Of course, I didn't realize I was carrying my past, and all that went along with it, to Bryan College."

> I TOTALLY FELT LIKE I WAS TRASH, NO-GOOD, BAD, COULDN'T DO ANYTHING RIGHT.

Things were better for Julie at Bryan, and a big reason for that was Julie spending focused time in God's Word. "When I got to Bryan, it was a different environment. Spiritually speaking, I was challenged more, and could really talk about God's Word with other students. That helped me see how the Bible related to me."

MARRIED LIFE

Soon after Julie arrived at college, she met Bob, an outgoing and popular senior, who was involved in many school activities. He and Julie hit it off right away and started dating. In a short time their relationship became serious. Bob proposed and Julie accepted. But almost immediately Julie started second-guessing her decision, to the point that she didn't think she could go through with the wedding.

"I knew Bob was going on to seminary to become a pastor, and even though I said yes to him, I didn't think I could do it. I couldn't become a pastor's wife because of how I felt about myself and my past. I felt so dirty and damaged. I felt different, really different from other people."

Julie and Bob weathered a few on-again, off-again decisions about their wedding but eventually got married after Bob's first year of seminary. Julie still wasn't settled, however. "My thinking at the time was, *Somehow I'll make it. Somehow I'll be this pastor's wife and just handle it.*"

Before they were married, Julie had told Bob about being sexually abused. He was the first person to know. It didn't change his feelings toward her, he said, and he still wanted to get married. Julie's abuse was no longer her secret, but she was still carrying a lot of unresolved emotional baggage.

Bob and Julie were only twenty-three and twenty when they got married. Bob was in his second year of seminary, and he and Julie lived in a one-bedroom mobile home on campus. Bob also began pastoring an out-of-state church the week after the wedding, so he was traveling back and forth on weekends. That first year was difficult, Julie said, but her outlook improved when she got pregnant.

"I just wanted to be a mom. I hadn't thought much about being a wife, but I had always loved children and wanted to be a mom. I felt like this was how, maybe, I could do good, you know? I could be good at loving children."

Bob and Julie eventually moved to a parsonage. They had two children and then adopted their third child, a boy. Their new son was hyperactive and had all kinds of struggles, which chipped away at Julie's already fragile emotions. "The added problems I was having with my son got me thinking, *Okay, now I can't even do this right.* At this point my mindset was, *I can't be a mother. I can't be a wife. I need to leave.*"

> I HAD ALWAYS LOVED CHILDREN AND WANTED TO BE A MOM.

As Julie described that period in her life, it was obvious more trouble was ahead. My concern grew stronger with her next statement.

"There was an older man in the church, and we developed a connection. He would stop by our house on his lunch hour. The first time, I think, it was to drop off something for Bob. Of course, Bob was hardly ever home during the day, so we'd sit and talk. That's basically how our relationship started."

Julie continued, "Then he started bringing little gifts. Next thing you know, he had convinced me that I needed to get out of my situation, and, of course, he was willing to help get me away."

Alarm bells were going off in my head as Julie talked about this "helpful" older man. But I hadn't heard her mention anything physical concerning the relationship, so I interrupted. "Was your relationship physical at this point, or was this just a friendship?"

"It wasn't just this kind gentleman that was helping me. No, he had ulterior motives. It wasn't good. It wasn't. He had a wife and was with his wife, but he got me a place to stay. There was nothing physical between us until I moved out. Then the affair started, and it lasted a couple of months."

I sensed Julie was feeling uncomfortable sharing an obviously painful event from her past. I was wondering if I should stop the interview, when she looked at me very sweetly and said, "This is difficult for me, but it's okay because I've talked about this before."

Julie paused, and then pressed on. "My kids were quite little at the time, and I just felt like they'd be better off without me in their lives. There was a part of me that wanted to die, but at the same time I wanted to be back with my kids. And then there came a point in the relationship where

I actually feared for my life. There were threats and guns involved, and that's when I made the decision that I was done with this game."

Julie told me, "I remember thinking, *This is all about me, it's not about anybody else, and I have to take responsibility and do the right thing.* So I called Bob. I told him I wanted to come back, and that I had made the decision to do what's right but understood if he didn't want me back or with my kids.

> **AT THAT MOMENT, I FELT VERY SAFE, AND PROBABLY FOR THE FIRST TIME I FELT LOVED.**

"Bob told me, 'You come back. We need you. We want you. And I'm not putting any conditions on you, saying you have to do this or that.'"

When Julie said this, my first thought was, *Wow! What an incredible loving response.* And as I thought about it a little longer, it dawned on me that Bob had modeled and extended Christ-like love to Julie. And his demonstration of love didn't end there.

Julie stated, "I remember Bob taking me in his arms and just saying, 'I love you.' I wasn't sure how to respond, because with my past, it was difficult for me to accept love from anybody. That took a while for me to work through. But at that moment, I felt very safe, and probably for the first time I felt loved."

At this point in her story, Julie reached out and started tapping, actually kind of pounding, her Bible, which was laying on the table in front of her. "And that's when this came into play so much."

LISTENING TO GOD

Julie explained, "I didn't even know where to start regarding Scripture. Yet I felt like the psalms had been so precious to me, so I started reading them. Psalm 51 was one that I practically memorized at that time, because in my mind, I was David, I guess.

> [1] *Have mercy on me, O God, according to*
> *your steadfast love;*
>
> *according to your abundant mercy blot out*
> *my transgressions.*
>
> [2] *Wash me thoroughly from my iniquity, and*
> *cleanse me from my sin!*
>
> [3] *For I know my transgressions, and my sin is*
> *ever before me.*
>
> [4] *Against you, you only, have I sinned and*
> *done what is evil in your sight,*
>
> *so that you may be justified in your words*
> *and blameless in your judgment.*
>
> [5] *Behold, I was brought forth in iniquity,*
> *and in sin did my mother conceive me.*

⁶*Behold, you delight in truth in the inward being, and you teach me wisdom in the secret heart.*

⁷*Purge me with hyssop, and I shall be clean; wash me, and I shall be whiter than snow.*

⁸*Let me hear joy and gladness; let the bones that you have broken rejoice.*

⁹*Hide your face from my sins, and blot out all my iniquities.*

¹⁰*Create in me a clean heart, O God, and renew a right spirit within me.*

¹¹*Cast me not away from your presence, and take not your Holy Spirit from me.*

¹²*Restore to me the joy of your salvation, and uphold me with a willing spirit.*

¹³*Then I will teach transgressors your ways, and sinners will return to you.*

¹⁴*Deliver me from bloodguiltiness, O God, O God of my salvation, and my tongue will sing aloud of your righteousness.*

¹⁵*O Lord, open my lips, and my mouth will declare your praise.*

¹⁶*For you will not delight in sacrifice, or I would give it; you will not be pleased with a burnt offering.*

> [17]*The sacrifices of God are a broken spirit;*
> *a broken and contrite heart, O God, you*
> *will not despise.*
>
> [18]*Do good to Zion in your good pleasure;*
> *build up the walls of Jerusalem;*
>
> [19]*then will you delight in right sacrifices,*
> *in burnt offerings and whole burnt*
> *offerings;*
> *then bulls will be offered on your altar.*

—Psalm 51 (esv)

Julie continued, "Also important was 1 John 1:9—'If we confess our sins, he is faithful and just to forgive us our sins and to cleanse us from all unrighteousness'—and picturing that cleansing and realizing that I was clean. *I was clean.* I cry almost every time I read that verse. These kinds of passages made me just want to get into the Word more."

I understood exactly what Julie was saying about certain passages drawing us in and back to God's Word. A number of passages in the psalms are especially meaningful to me. Three that I return to frequently are Psalm 25:1-5, Psalm 63:1-8, and Psalm 139. They are comforting and remind me of God's love for me and how every detail of my life is in His hands.

Julie's face brightened as she shared that Bob also played a big role in her taking in and learning about Scripture. "When Bob was preparing sermons, he'd come to me with passages and tell me his thoughts, and we'd really discuss God's Word. That was so fun. We still do that today. He'll bring up a passage, or I'll find something that I get excited about, and we'll talk through and consider it together. I love doing that."

I asked Julie, "What else are you doing now, one-on-one with God and His Word?" She was quick to tell me she wasn't a traditional journaler, but she did have a thing for 3-by-5 cards.

She explained, "Something I do on my own is to write verses on notecards. I typically do that when I'm having my devotions and there's a verse that really stands out to me. I'll write the verse on one side of the card, and on the back side I'll write a prayer that somehow ties to the verse. Then I put the card on my refrigerator or maybe in my purse."

Before saying another word, Julie reached down and started digging around in her purse. Within a few seconds, her hand rose exuberantly in the air holding a 3-by-5 note-card. She told me she'd written it earlier that week. I smiled, and asked if she would read it to me.

"Psalm 27:4," she started. "'The one thing I ask of the Lord . . . is to live in the house of the Lord all the days of my life, delighting in the Lord's perfections and meditating in his temple' (NLT). And then on the back, the prayer I wrote said, 'Lord God, make me beautiful inside and out today as you work through me to love and serve those around me.'"

I liked it. Using notecards for key verses and prayer made a lot of sense to me. Plus, it was simple and quick. I could definitely see myself doing this. I wanted to know a little more, though, about Julie's approach to Bible reading.

"Sometimes I'm involved in a Bible study, but other times I simply read books of the Bible, and when I do, I don't read a set amount each day. If I'm reading through the book of James, for example, I might read two chapters or I might read half of a chapter, depending on what I find there. And when I see something that touches me and I want to remember it, I copy it down on a card. Writing it down emphasizes the verse for me and helps me learn and remember it better."

SOMETHING I DO ON MY OWN IS TO WRITE VERSES ON NOTECARDS.

I was also curious if Julie had any favorite books of the Bible. Without hesitation, she responded, "The whole book of Philippians, but my favorite chapter is chapter 4. It talks a lot about the joy of the Lord and joy that we can have. Strangely enough, before I worked through some of my issues, my favorite verse was Philippians 4:4, 'Rejoice in the Lord always.' Looking back, I would quote that verse to people, yet I didn't live it out."

When I asked why, Julie replied, "It was probably because I wanted it so badly. But you know, I can look at that verse now, actually all of chapter 4, and say, 'It's real, I've got it, I've got it.'"

Julie's voice was so confident as she spoke those words. Her obvious trust in God's Word brought a smile to my face. I felt led to ask, "What does the Bible mean to you today?"

"So much. It's my guide, my constant. You know it is truth and that nothing changes. It's a part of who I am, and I depend on it."

JULIE TODAY

Bob and Julie reuniting, combined with Julie's decision to get into the Word, was truly the turning point for Julie. She still had plenty of issues she needed to deal with, but she had finally taken that big first step, and Bob was there supporting and encouraging her along the way. And, of course, God was with her, too.

Julie told me, "It was a long process of God healing my heart, my dealing with things, and learning that I needed to take responsibility for my actions."

Bob and Julie's marriage continued to grow stronger and stronger with time, and today, their love and dedication to each other is obvious. (I actually got the opportunity to spend a little time with Julie and Bob together over lunch, and it was a treat.) Bob has pastored a number of churches over the years with Julie by his side, teaching women's studies and helping do many things in the church.

I was so pleased to hear that eventually Julie was able to tell her story to others and is using it today to help other women see how God loves and cares for them, and that His desire is for each of us to know Him personally.

WHAT WE CAN LEARN FROM JULIE'S STORY

+ **Forgiveness is a must for a healthy relationship.**
  Forgiveness and restoration go hand in hand. We saw that clearly in Julie's story. Bob's unconditional offer of forgiveness to Julie, and Julie's acceptance of his offer were pivotal to the restoration of their marriage. All relationships (marriage, family, friendships, work, church) are difficult. Conflict happens, words get spoken hastily, we act rashly based on emotions, and before you know it, people are damaged and the relationship is broken. So it's crucial that we embrace forgiveness—offering it even when the offending party may not deserve it, and accepting it when we've wronged someone else. Ephesians 4:32 tells us, "Be kind to one another, tenderhearted, forgiving one another, as God in Christ forgave you."

+ **Our painful experiences can help others.** The sexual abuse Julie endured for many years was awful. There's no question she suffered emotional and spiritual harm. Yet God healed her, and Julie is now using her story to reach out to women, letting them know about God's love and the healing that comes from having a personal relationship with Christ and spending time in God's Word.

+ **All of us have had painful experiences of some sort, and we may be able to help someone else as a result.** When I finally decided to start talking about my problems with anxiety, I was shocked at how many people would tell me that they were suffering with panic attacks and fear, and how my talking about how God helped me through that situation, helped them. So don't automatically bury your painful situations away. Maybe you can use them to help someone else.

+ **Where our minds dwell, we will likely go.** Our minds are powerful. So when we think about something that tempts us over and over, or we continue to dwell on negative thoughts, we are likely to give in. Julie convincing herself that she needed to leave Bob is a good example. If we fill our minds with God's truth, we will be less likely to succumb to temptation. Philippians 4:8 says, "Finally, brothers, whatever is true, whatever is honorable, whatever is just, whatever is pure, whatever is lovely, whatever is commendable, if there is any excellence, if there is anything worthy of praise, think about these things."

+ **Women must handle relationships with men carefully.** People don't typically set out to have an affair, but we all know they happen—a lot. Julie's relationship with the older man from her church started out innocently enough, but it didn't take long for this relationship to change into one that was first unhealthy, and then inappropriate. Her story provides a good reminder of how vulnerable and susceptible we are when we're discontented, unhappy, or feeling unfulfilled. Because of this, we need to be extra careful to protect ourselves and our marriages.

RESPONDING TO GOD'S WORD

Julie said her favorite book of the Bible is Philippians, so that's what we're going to explore and consider. There were two things about engaging God's Word that I took away from my talk with Julie. First was how helpful it was for Julie to discuss and consider passages with Bob, and second was Julie using notecards to write down Scripture verses that were meaningful to her and then her corresponding prayers. So we're going to try both. I'll go first and talk about my experience. Then it's your turn.

> IF WE FILL OUR MINDS WITH GOD'S TRUTH, WE WILL BE LESS LIKELY TO SUCCUMB TO TEMPTATION.

TAMI'S PHILIPPIANS EXPERIENCE

Discuss and Consider:

I asked my husband, Jeff, if he would read Philippians and then discuss chapters or portions of chapters with me in the evenings. He agreed and we set a start date. I had forgotten, however, that Jeff's father, Dean, was coming to stay with us that week. I considered postponing our start, but then decided we should include him. Dean is ninety-six, by the way, and I wasn't sure how this would go, but *why not?* He ended up being a nice addition to our talk and study time.

As I left for work I reminded Jeff and his dad to read Philippians and told them we'd discuss the first chapter that evening. As soon as the dishes were cleared from our evening meal, we began. I pulled up Philippians 1 on my iPad and set that before Dean. He was a bit startled because he'd never used an iPad, but he caught on. Jeff and I used our Bibles.

We began by reading Philippians 1 out loud so everyone would have it fresh in their minds. I was the designated reader. When I got about ten verses in, Dean stopped me saying that he was having a hard time taking in so much Scripture at once. That was good to know, so we decided to only discuss the first few verses in this sitting.

I finished reading the chapter, and then went back to Paul's greeting in verses 1 and 2. The first question we asked was: What information is there in these verses that would be helpful for us as we read Philippians? Right away Jeff responded, "Paul is writing this to the church." And then we talked about how the word "saints" revealed that Paul was writing to people who were Christ-followers. The way he spoke in this book would be different than in other parts of the New Testament where some people hearing the message didn't know Christ. Next we moved on to verses 3 through 5, noting Paul's thankfulness for other believers supporting him in ministry. Then our focus turned to verses 6 through 8, with a short discussion about the "good works" being done by these Philippian believers and Paul's affection for them. We then considered Paul's words about having knowledge and discernment and being filled with righteousness through Jesus Christ.

We wrapped up our discussion time with this question: "Who supported you spiritually that you are thankful for?" Dean perked up immediately and shared something neither Jeff nor I had ever heard. "When I was in the war," he said, "there were twelve faithful ladies who would meet at the church every day and pray for the local boys who were in the war. I can picture them in my mind, all dressed in black and sitting at the front of the church. They would send me letters telling me that they prayed specifically for me. And that meant so much. I used to tell my army buddies as we went to sleep at night, 'I know I'm going to wake up in the morning because I'm prayed for and God is watching over me.' And in the morning when I woke up I'd say, 'See, I told you. I'm covered.' I am so thankful for those twelve women."

I was moved by Dean's participation in our group and pleased that what we read and talked about not only helped him recall a precious memory, but showed us the impact of receiving and giving spiritual support. Jeff closed our time with a short prayer, thanking God for people who have supported us spiritually and asking God to help us be intentional in returning the favor to others.

A couple of nights later, we had visitors who spent the night at our house. I didn't want to break our routine, so I asked the couple to join us. They did, and it was great. So, go ahead and be creative as you seek others out to discuss Philippians.

Notecard Verse: Philippians 1:20 stood out to me as we read chapter 1 in Philippians, so I selected it as my notecard verse: "It is my eager expectation and hope that I will not be at all ashamed, but that with full courage now as always Christ will be honored in my body, whether by life or death."

On the back of my notecard, I wrote this prayer: "Lord, help me to represent You *boldly*. Help me to speak freely, to declare You and demonstrate Your love to those around me."

POST-PHILIPPIANS THOUGHTS

It was a treat to read through and consider Philippians with my husband and father-in-law. Being able to verbalize my thoughts and feelings is helpful for me, because it often clarifies my thinking. In addition, discussion often prompts someone else to jump in and add information, fine tune the point made, add in a supporting passage, or even provide a personal example.

Those are things I wouldn't have access to on my own.

Another good thing about our group approach was that it made me spend more time considering each verse than if I had simply read it on my own and written down some of my thoughts. With three people, we were all spending time considering not only our thoughts, but the points and questions made by the others. So the overall experience was richer and fuller.

One drawback was that I was the designated organizer of the group. In other words, I was the one making sure everyone was reading and finding the time to sit down together and then actually prompting everyone to turn off the television or put down their book and come to the table for study time. It wasn't too difficult because my group was in my house, but when a group consists of people outside your house, friends for example, it does require some managing and directing. I've headed up a number of small study groups with friends, and even though there is extra responsibility, it is *totally* worth the effort.

So now it's your turn. Find someone, or a few people, with whom you can read through Philippians. It could be your husband or boyfriend. It could be a sister, brother, or parent. It could be a friend. And if the person you want to read and study with doesn't live near you, connect over the phone or maybe through Skype. You set your own schedule. You don't have to talk daily, and you can meet wherever you want. Have fun learning together!

"At camp was the first time

I had heard the Gospel

and about grace and

that you don't have to earn

your way to heaven.

I was so excited," she said.

With a hint of a twinkle

in her eye, Angie added,

"That night I got the

best 'bath' of my life."

CHAPTER 7

GOD'S WORD, OUR LIFELINE:

ANGIE'S STORY

"I was at the point where all I could do is take the next step, just the next step, and have the faith to finish that day. And throughout this experience, the Scriptures that I had memorized really anchored me and kept me focused on the truth—not my emotions, not the circumstances, which we all know can literally fall apart in five seconds."

ANGIE IS WHAT most people would call a glass half-full person. I would go further and say she's a glass overflowing person! I love that about her.

I've known Angie for quite a few years. We used to attend the same church and sing in choir together. As far back as I can remember, she has been full of energy and on fire for the Lord. She is most certainly a people person, and a contagious energy just radiates from Angie. She has a way of making you feel accepted and welcome.

Angie is married to John, who is fun to be around and an incredible golf instructor (yes, he's given me lessons). They have three grown children. Angie teaches at a Christian school, which is probably why she loves to learn and help others do the same, and she is very involved with her church.

Angie and I got the opportunity to spend a few hours together talking about some of her life experiences and her recent battle with ovarian cancer. As I listened to Angie, it was evident that she has had a long and steady relationship with the Lord.

ANGIE'S STORY

From a very early age, Angie was aware and mindful of God. She was raised Catholic, and remembers having a huge sense of guilt and a great fear of God. "I would lay in bed at night worrying about going to hell if I died, because I knew I wasn't good enough," she told me.

It wasn't until Angie attended a Christian camp that she fully understood God's love for her and learned about His free gift of salvation.

"At camp was the first time I had heard the Gospel and about grace and that you don't have to earn your way to heaven. I was so excited," she said. With a hint of a twinkle in her eye, Angie added, "That night I got the best 'bath' of my life." I had a feeling where Angie was going with her story, but wasn't exactly sure. She continued, "I got in the empty bathtub with all my clothes on and sat with my counselor and asked her questions about Jesus for three hours. That's where I got saved. Isn't that awesome?"

I had to smile, because I think Angie was almost as excited telling me about her bathtub experience as she was on the actual night years earlier. She was beaming as she recalled getting saved, and I loved it.

Exuberantly, Angie continued, "After that, I was so fired up to tell everybody what had happened to me and about God's free gift of salvation—that it's nothing we can earn, that it's not about being good enough and we don't have to do anything."

I WAS SO FIRED UP TO TELL EVERYBODY WHAT HAD HAPPENED TO ME AND ABOUT GOD'S FREE GIFT OF SALVATION.

Amen. Preach it, sister! is what I was thinking as I took in Angie's passion for sharing Christ with others.

LISTENING TO AND LEARNING FROM GOD

Then Angie switched gears a little and began talking about getting into the Bible. "I also had a hunger to learn. I got hold of a Navigators packet with an article that talked about memorizing Scripture. That got me started memorizing."

Angie was also attending a Young Life youth group, but when her leaders moved away, she struggled (actually, she described it to me as "floundered") for the next four years. Even so, she kept reading her Bible. "I tried to read every day, but it wasn't always making sense to me."

I was struck by Angie's determination. So often when we're struggling spiritually or we lose contact with another Christian who is a strong spiritual influence, we give up on Bible reading or stop going to church or fall away from God. Not Angie. She continued to press forward and pursue God.

In college, Angie continued to memorize verses and share her faith with others. "I can still recall some of those verses," she said. "They were so fundamental in developing my relationship with Jesus."

At this point, Angie was operating as a "lone" Christian, and by herself she just couldn't get the spiritual nourishment she needed. Thankfully, she found a Bible-teaching church that provided the perfect environment for her to take in God's Word and grow spiritually. "I could hardly wait for church. I took notes like crazy and learned as much as I possibly could. And I'm one of those people that if I learn it, I have to share it. I can't learn something and then just sit there."

> THE WHOLE TIME I WAS HANGING ON TO MY BIBLE, LEARNING MORE AND MORE SCRIPTURES. IT WAS MY LIFELINE.

From Angie's tone, it was clear she couldn't fathom why someone wouldn't share Christ. I, too, am a firm believer in sharing Christ and talking to people about the Bible and God whenever opportunities present themselves. But as I pointed out to Angie, that's not the norm. While most Christ-followers agree that sharing their faith is important, only a small percentage actually get out and do it.

Angie seemed a bit surprised. "I could hardly wait to get it out of my lips, because it was the most exciting thing ever. My thinking was, *Why would you want to keep that to yourself?*"

Angie talked about being in her early twenties and married at this point in her life. "I was so unchurched and untaught in the Scriptures, I didn't even realize my husband wasn't saved because he gave all the right answers, and I just believed him." A few years into the marriage, Angie discovered that her husband was having an affair. She was pregnant with their first child. The relationship ended in a nasty divorce. It was difficult, but Angie held fast to God and His Word.

I was touched by Angie's description of her dependence on God. "The whole time I was hanging on to my Bible, learning more and more Scriptures. It was my lifeline. The Scriptures really spoke to me. They were a comfort and a place of refuge. I knew it was an anchor and that even if my husband left me, God wasn't going to forsake me."

Angie then fast-forwarded a few years to when she met her second husband, John. I assumed John was a Christian, because I know John now, and he's a strong believer, but Angie told me otherwise.

"When John and I started dating, I asked him about his beliefs and he said, 'Well, of course, I'm a Christian, I grew up in America.'" Angie paused and gave me a knowing look, then continued, "And I'm like (imitates the sound of a buzzer), *Wrong answer!* I told him, 'I'll marry you if you're walking with Christ. I'm not going to marry somebody who is not crazy about Jesus.' I really meant that. I was willing to be alone because I was satisfied with my son and with Jesus."

As John and Angie dated, John did eventually receive Christ as his Savior. Not long after that, they decided to get married. So at the age of twenty-nine, Angie married John, and they hit the ground running, choosing to have a baby in their first year of marriage. As more children followed, Angie quit her teaching job to be a stay-at-home mom.

"We could barely make ends meet," she recalled. "So I did all kinds of things to help our financial situation. I baked my own bread, I hung other people's wall paper, I sewed and ironed for people."

God's Word had been so crucial to Angie up to this point, so I was curious and asked, "What was your relationship with God like now that you had four kids to take care of? Were you still memorizing Scripture?" Angie's answer surprised me.

"I was disciplined, because I was going to a Bible study every week, and (Angie was emphatic here) *I had to have that lesson done.* The rest of the week I would improvise because it's seriously difficult to get uninterrupted time when you have little ones. Some days, I may not have opened my Bible. Other days, I might have been in it, off and on, for ten minutes here, five minutes there."

I jumped in. "So what exactly were you doing? Give me some examples."

Angie responded, "I discovered that if I taped a verse to the mirror or put Bibles in different rooms where I knew I was going to be nursing a baby, for example, I would typically read my Bible. I had Bibles all over the place so I could just pick one up and start reading wherever I was in the house."

Being the planner that I am, I was impressed by Angie's intentionality to make sure she didn't neglect God's Word. And what she described any of us could put into practice—children not required.

A CONSTANT THEME

A constant theme with Angie was memorizing Scripture. This is not something I regularly do, although I have memorized Scripture off and on at different times. So I wanted to hear about how Angie memorized. My assumption was she had an organized plan or a set number of verses to be memorized per week. But that wasn't her approach at all.

"What I memorize depends on what I'm reading," she said. "I always pray about what I'm supposed to learn from

God and ask Him to make those things jump off the page." At this point, Angie reached over and patted her purse. "I keep a little spiral-bound notecard packet with me—in fact, I have one in my purse right now—and if a verse jumps off the page, I'll write it down. I don't worry about when I'm going to memorize it."

Angie then added, "I also read a lot of Christian books, and sometimes what I'm reading will direct me to Scriptures that I want to memorize. So I've got all these verses I know God wants me to look at. Plus, there's a going-back process. I need to review verses I've already memorized or I will start forgetting them."

TEACHING CHILDREN

Angie and I took a quick break to get a refill on our coffee and then jumped back to discussing Scripture memorization. Somehow our conversation turned to Angie encouraging her kids to memorize. I was intrigued. Angie actually began this when her children were babies by simply reading Scripture out loud so they would hear her voice saying God's Word. When the kids got a little older, Angie used music to help each child focus on and remember key verses.

I'm a huge music person, so I asked Angie to tell me more about the music.

Smiling, she replied, "I found that the way they learned best was if we sang the Scripture verse." Without any warning, Angie enthusiastically started singing Ephesians 4:32: "Be kind, one to another . . ." Can you picture it? We're in the middle of a restaurant and Angie is singing Scripture. Of course I was smiling because this is just Angie. When she stopped singing, she said, "You know, my kids can all sing them to this day."

I didn't recognize the melody, so asked, "Did you make up that tune?"

"Yes, I just made it up. Silly ones. And when we'd really struggle with something in our home, I would think, *Okay, let's get a Scripture out and learn a verse about this.* And what's kind of funny is even today my kids tell me, 'Mom, you sang everything, and we can remember all those songs. You should have taught us more.' They were just ditties, little tunes like 'Row, Row, Row Your Boat' that I'd adapt to Scripture to help them remember it. And, honestly, it's a great way to memorize even as an adult."

> I ALWAYS PRAY ABOUT WHAT I'M SUPPOSED TO LEARN FROM GOD AND ASK HIM TO MAKE THOSE THINGS JUMP OFF THE PAGE.

I loved how Angie was so proactive about laying a biblical foundation for her kids. Even so, she and John went through some difficult times with the kids as teenagers, especially when one of their daughters tried to commit suicide. God and His Word sustained John and Angie through this horrific valley. And all those verses Angie had memorized over the years were invaluable to her.

"I don't know where I would have been without God's Word ready in my mind to fight against the enemy who

I DON'T KNOW WHERE I WOULD HAVE BEEN WITHOUT GOD'S WORD READY IN MY MIND TO FIGHT AGAINST THE ENEMY.

was trying to totally destroy me, our marriage, our family," she said. "I was at the point where all I could do is take the next step, just the next step, and have the faith to finish that day. And throughout this experience, the Scriptures that I had memorized really anchored me and kept me focused on the truth—not my emotions, not the circumstances, which we all know can literally fall apart in five seconds."

SCRIPTURE AND CANCER

At this point in our conversation, Angie and I moved forward a few years to Angie's bout with ovarian cancer. She shared, "Right before I got cancer, I was really challenged by God—I sensed He was asking me, 'Are you willing to give me everything?' I told Him, *'Yes, Lord, what would I not give You? I'm giving You my kids, I'm giving You my marriage, I'm giving You our finances. I don't know what else You want Lord, but whatever You want, take it, because I belong to You and I'm here to serve You.'* Next thing you know, my doctor tells me he thinks we need to take a cyst off my ovary. And what was supposed to be a forty-five minute surgery, ended up taking five and a half hours because I was full of tumors."

When Angie woke up from surgery, she learned about the tumors and was told she probably had cancer. John and the kids asked Angie what she thought about everything. Angie's response? "Whatever God wants to do with my life, He can do it. He knows it, I know it, and whatever happens, it's okay with me.

"Everybody was looking at me like I must still be drugged out from surgery, but I was fine. I told them, 'Why shouldn't it be okay? Why should we only take the blessings and then be angry if things don't go our way? I can't believe this isn't God's best for me. Whether I live or whether I die, I win either way. I can't lose. This is a win-win situation.'"

When I heard Angie say her cancer was a "win-win," memories of my husband's bout with cancer flooded my mind. A few weeks into chemotherapy and much sickness, he had said the same thing to me. They were both right, but as the person who isn't the sick one, sometimes it's hard to hear.

"Cancer was never horrible for me," Angie said, "because, again, I could look back at the Scriptures God had me memorize, and they were gold to me. When I would start saying 'what if . . .' or 'what about . . . ,' I would just stop and tell myself, *I'm not going there. I'm going to live in this moment, right now, and see what God has for me.* And it's because of knowing and memorizing God's Word that I could do that."

One particularly helpful passage to Angie as she battled cancer was Deuteronomy 31:8: "The Lord is the one who goes ahead of you; He will be with you. He will not fail you or forsake you. Do not fear or be dismayed" (NASB). With confidence in her voice, Angie told me, "That verse was my strength on many days, because I knew God was going ahead of me and there was no reason to be dismayed. There was no reason for fear. None."

ANGIE'S STUDY TIME

I had learned a lot about Scripture memorization, but I also wanted to know about Angie's current routine. She told me, "I get up half an hour early, so I'll have at least thirty minutes. Sometimes it ends up being longer than that, and sometimes it's shorter. If I feel the Lord and I are done, I'm done. But then later, when I take a walk, I'll memorize or contemplate what I read earlier." Angie paused, before adding, "You've got to take time to digest what you've read. This is as important as memorization."

Angie is flexible, though, with her routine, and will deviate from her normal reading from time to time to focus on a particular verse or passage if it's really been on her mind. "I look at the meanings of words, and figure out how they relate to each other," she explained. "I consider things like, 'What am I supposed to do with this Lord? Why have You put this on my heart? What do You want to change about me? What do I need to be more sensitive to because of this Scripture?'

And then I'll also work on memorizing it."

Since Angie brought up memorization again, I asked about her process.

"I'm a visual learner, but I'm also kinesthetic, so I love to walk as I memorize. I figured out a long time ago that I memorize better when I walk or repeat the words in some kind of a rhythm, or even put a verse to music like I did with my kids. Those types of things help me to lock the words in my memory."

The thought of memorizing Scripture can be a little daunting, scary, overwhelming (you pick your own word), so I asked Angie, "What would you say to someone who is skeptical about memorizing Scripture?"

She thought for a moment, and then delivered this wonderful response. "A lot of people are scared of trying to memorize scripture. They think they can't do it. They'll tell you they don't memorize well. You know none of us really do, but when you make the decision to do it, the Holy Spirit will help you. You don't do this by yourself."

She continued, "Memorizing God's Word has made all the difference to me. I've been in a bazillion Bible studies, but there is nothing that will change you like memorizing Scripture. It's like receiving an infusion of God—that transfusion of His blood, of His mercy, of His grace literally changes and transforms us."

WHAT WE CAN LEARN FROM ANGIE'S STORY

+ **Engaging God's Word is fundamental for growth.** Angie provided a clear picture of how engaging God's Word (receiving, reflecting on, and responding to it) is fundamental to growing in our relationship with God and, in turn, growing spiritually. God speaks to us through His Word, the Bible. And engaging the Bible is the primary way we get to know His heart, His mind, what He desires for our lives. So if we want to grow spiritually, we have to be in His Word.

+ **Knowing God's Word equips us to share Christ.** God expects us to tell others about Christ. Mark 16:15 says, "And he said to them, 'Go into all the world and proclaim the gospel to the whole creation.'" (See also Matthew 5:13–16; 1 Chronicles 16:23–24; Matthew 28:18–20; Luke 24:46–47; and Romans 10:9–15.) And He's given us His Word to equip and empower us to do just that. So the more we take in God's Word, the more likely we'll be to talk about God, the Bible, and Jesus with others. When I asked Angie how she was able to be so bold about sharing her faith, she said, "It was the Scripture I'd memorized that gave me the confidence. It wasn't me. It's that joy of knowing the Word, of having it be part of who you are. It changes the way you view situations. Without that arsenal of truth embedded in me, I didn't have the confidence to do it."

+ **Growing spiritually requires intentionality.**
Spiritual growth requires action on our part. It
will not just happen. That means we have to
be intentional and plan time to be in the Bible.
If our approach is waiting until we think we'll
have time or until we feel like reading, it will
rarely, if ever, happen. And I'm speaking from
experience. If I'm not intentional about spending time in the Word and planning a specific
time for that to happen, other activities will
push that time with God right out of my day.

+ **God and His Word must be a priority.** We
each have twenty-four hours to use every day.
Where in that twenty-four hours will you re-
serve uninterrupted time to spend with God
each day?

+ **God's Word must be passed on to the next
generation.** It's critical for us to pass on God's
Word to our children, grandchildren, nieces,
nephews, and other young people in our lives.
I was so fortunate to be brought up in a Bible-
centered, Christian home. For as long as I can
remember my parents taught me about God,
the Bible, and Jesus, and when the doors to our
church were open, we were there. That teaching
and modeling played a huge role in who I am
and where I am today. I can only wonder what
my life would be like and where I would be spiritually today if I hadn't received godly teaching
and instruction from my parents. (Proverbs
22:6: "Train up a child in the way he should
go; even when he is old he will not depart from

it." See also Psalm 78:1–8 and Deuteronomy 4:5–10.)

+ **God's Word strengthens us through storms.** Difficult situations and hard times are a given. They will come into your life. So it's important to know God's Word and have it stored in your heart. Then, when one of those storms roll in, you don't have to worry and search for strength, comfort, guidance, and peace because God's Word is already providing it. We saw this demonstrated over and over in Angie's story. The Scriptures she had memorized sustained her through divorce, a suicidal child, and cancer. What a motivator for us to make sure we're taking in and memorizing God's Word, so we will be better prepared for our next storm.

RESPONDING TO GOD'S WORD

No doubt about it, Angie is passionate about memorizing Scripture. So our goal is to get passionate about it, too. Angie's favorite book of the Bible is Isaiah, and she particularly likes chapter 55. So we're going to initially read through and consider Isaiah 55, asking God to reveal what He has for us from these verses. Then, as we're reading Isaiah 55 we'll follow Angie's model of looking for a verse (or more) to memorize. Once you find the verse or verses you want to memorize (from Isaiah 55 or another passage altogether), write them down and begin. But keep in mind that the way Angie memorized may be different than the way you or I memorize. The important thing is doing what works for you so that you will be able to remember and draw on that Scripture when you need it in the future.

TAMI'S ISAIAH 55 EXPERIENCE

I read through Isaiah 55 once and then decided to go back and read it again, this time writing down observations and specific things in Isaiah 55 that stood out to me. Here's what I recorded.

Verse 1: *"Everyone who thirsts." This is a total call to mankind, no favorites, no preconditions. My study Bible used the word "universal."*

Thought that was a good word. This is a free offering from God.

Verse 2: *"Delight yourself" in rich food. Shows me I should be delighting in God and His Word. How am I accomplishing this?*

"Eat what is good." Again, what is good? God's Word. Lets me know that only God satisfies.

Verse 6: *An immediate call to act now, because we may not get another opportunity. We could be killed, Christ could return. There is urgency here. Do Not Wait.*

Verse 7: *God wants to forgive us. "He will abundantly pardon" shows compassion and love.*

Verse 11: *God's Word is powerful and active. It impacts and changes lives.*

Verses 12–13: *Picture of complete joy. Love the description of hills singing and the trees clapping their hands.*

Memorization: I decided to memorize both verses 10 and 11. While I would have preferred to memorize just one verse, I felt like verse 11 by itself wasn't as powerful. So even though the two verses together were more challenging, it's where I landed.

> [10] *For as the rain and the snow come down from heaven and do not return there but water the earth,*
>
> *making it bring forth and sprout,*
>
> *giving seed to the sower and bread to the eater,*
>
> [11] *so shall my word be that goes out from my mouth;*
>
> *it shall not return to me empty,*
>
> *but it shall accomplish that which I purpose,*
>
> *and shall succeed in the thing for which I sent it.*
>
> —Isaiah 55:10–11

I used what I would call a practical approach for memorizing verse 10, drawing on my knowledge of rain and snow to help me to remember what the writer is describing. Then, once I got verse 10 down, I moved on to that powerful verse 11.

Memorizing for me happens by simply repeating phrases over and over. I begin with one phrase and then add more as I'm able. I find it especially helpful to say the verse out loud as I'm trying to learn it. That way I'm taking it in using two senses instead of just one. When I get to a point where I feel fairly confident, I'll seek out my husband to listen and make sure I'm reciting the passage correctly.

Fortunately for me, memorizing comes fairly easily. That's just the way God has wired my brain. But I realize that isn't the case for everyone. So if you don't get your verse memorized immediately, that's okay. Stay with it, working on the verse phrase by phrase or pieces at a time. Then, once you get it, keep going back and reciting it for several days to really impress it into your memory.

POST-ISAIAH 55 THOUGHTS

I loved what God showed me in Isaiah 55. It is such a rich chapter that I actually read the chapters around it, as well. It was a good reminder for me that I need to be more intentional about spending time in some of the lengthier books of the Old Testament, such as Isaiah, Job, Jeremiah, and Ezekiel.

And what are my thoughts on memorizing? I needed this assignment, and I need to do more. Memorizing is something I have not spent a lot of time doing. Yet, when I have taken the time and memorized, it has been meaningful at the time and helpful later when I drew on those words to help me in a situation or help someone else. So the question I have to ask myself is, *Why am I not memorizing?* And the answer is, *I've been lazy.* So, going forward I have a new goal—to memorize one verse each week. How about you? Will you join me?

CONCLUSION
THE BIBLE IS FOR YOU!

WE DID IT! I trust that as you read the stories of each of the women featured in this book, and then tried their favorite way of engaging God's Word, that you spent time with God in a fresh way and got to know Him better.

How you choose to go forward from here is up to you. Whatever approach you prefer—one you used before or one you discovered here or perhaps a mixture of both—keep using it to regularly spend time with God, receiving, reflecting on, and responding to His Word.

God loves you and created you to be in relationship with Him. So stay in His Word, anticipating and listening for God to speak powerfully to your heart and draw you ever closer to Him.

PSALM 119 STUDY

As a committed Bible engager, one of my favorite reads is Psalm 119, because almost every verse reveals something to us about God's Word. I like to refer to this psalm as "the Bible engagement psalm."

A while back I decided to spend some concentrated time reading through and considering Psalm 119 with the specific goal of understanding more about God and the importance of His Word in my life. The exercise was well worth the effort. I learned a lot, and thought you might find it beneficial as well.

Psalm 119 is the longest chapter in the Bible, coming in at 176 verses. But don't let that put you off because it's divided into twenty-two stanzas, each containing eight verses, which makes it easily readable over multiple days.

My approach to Psalm 119 was stanza by stanza. I did not have a set amount of verses I wanted to read each day. I wanted the freedom to spend as much time on one stanza as I wanted. So some days I would only focus on one stanza, and other days I'd work through several, based on what God was showing me on that particular day. I used a three-step approach:

Step 1. The first thing I do is simply read through the selected stanza to take in and familiarize myself with the text.

Step 2. Then, I go back and read the eight verses again, with this specific question in mind: *What does this reveal to me about God?* My second read-through is a slow one because I stop to reflect after each phrase or verse. As I work through the text, I write down everything that comes to mind, sometimes re-reading a verse several times.

Step 3. Step three is to again read the selected stanza. This time, though, I consider this question: *What does this show me about God's Word?* Just as before, this is a slow, deliberate read as I contemplate what I am taking in and what God is showing me. Again, I write down everything that stands out, and read some of the verses several times as part of the process.

To enhance your understanding of who God is and the importance of His Word, I encourage you to work through Psalm 119, trying the three-step study process above. As you start each day, ask God for His understanding and then jump in. And take your time. I am still surprised at how much more I see when I simply take a little extra time to go back and re-read verses.

To get the most benefit from this exercise, you really do need to write down what God is showing you. So make sure you have a notebook and pen with you as you begin each day, or if you prefer, type out what you're seeing on a tablet or your computer like I did. Then it's saved for you to share with someone else or for your own reference.

Have fun with Psalm 119! And thank you for engaging God's Word with me through *Off the Page & Into Your Life*.

APPENDIX

The Power of 4:

RESEARCH FROM THE CENTER FOR BIBLE ENGAGEMENT

FOR MORE THAN eight years, the Center for Bible Engagement has researched the spiritual lives of more than 100,000 people from around the world. The findings consistently show that engaging the Bible four or more days a week is the single most powerful predictor of spiritual growth.

Our conceptual definition of spiritual growth focuses on "becoming less of the person I was before I committed my life to following Jesus and more like Christ in my thoughts, words, and deeds." We use multiple measures of spiritual growth including moral behavior, emotional struggles, proactively living out the Christian faith, and self-perceived growth.

Key findings include:

+ If a person engages the Bible four or more times a week, their odds of giving in to temptations such as drinking to excess, viewing pornography, lashing out in anger, gossiping, and lying significantly decrease.

+ Receiving, reflecting on, and responding to God's Word four or more times a week decreases a person's odds of struggling with issues such as feeling bitter, thinking destructively about self or others, having difficulty forgiving others, and feeling discouraged.

+ Engaging Scripture produces a more proactive faith among Christians. Controlling for factors such as age, gender, church attendance, and prayer practices, the individual engaged in the Bible has significantly higher odds of giving financially, memorizing Scripture, and sharing their faith with others.

+ People's perceptions of their own spiritual growth are also impacted by how often they hear from God through the Bible. Those who engage Scripture most days of the week are less likely to feel spiritually stagnant and to feel that they can't please God.

In summary, the powerful effects of Bible engagement on spiritual growth have been reliably demonstrated across many studies. In addition, organizations such as the Willow Creek Association and Lifeway Research have reported similar findings, as well.

Together, these independent lines of research lead to one simple conclusion: Engaging the Bible most days of the week is critical for growth in the Christian faith. The implications of this conclusion are wide-reaching and profound for Christian pastors and leaders, churches, schools, and evangelistic ministries. Those serious about helping people grow in a relationship with Jesus Christ need to carefully consider where they are investing their energies, and if those activities are producing lifelong impacts by getting people engaged in the Word.

THE "FOUR TIMES PER WEEK" FACTOR

Across our thousands of surveys, we've repeatedly examined the relationship between spiritual practices, moral behavior, and struggles. Logistic regression analyses controlling for factors such as age, gender, church attendance, and prayer practices have consistently shown that Bible engagement uniquely predicts how often people give in to temptations and struggles.

Summarizing across all of the studies, we find that if a person engages the Bible four or more times a week, their odds of giving in to these temptations decreases:

⬇ Drinking to excess -62%

⬇ Viewing pornography -59%

⬇ Having sex outside marriage -59%

⬇ Gambling -45%

- ↓ Lashing out in anger -31%

- ↓ Gossiping -28%

- ↓ Lying -28%

- ↓ Neglecting family -26%

- ↓ Overeating or mishandling food -20%

- ↓ Overspending or mishandling money -20%

Bible engagement also produces more peace and joy in a person's life, by reducing the frequency of various emotional struggles. Receiving, reflecting on, and responding to God's Word four or more times a week decreases a person's odds of struggling with these issues:

- ↓ Feeling bitter -40%

- ↓ Thinking destructively about self or others -32%

- ↓ Feeling like they have to hide what they do or feel -32%

- ↓ Having difficulty forgiving others -31%

- ↓ Feeling discouraged -31%

- ↓ Experiencing loneliness -30%

- ↓ Having difficulty forgiving oneself -26%

- ↓ Overeating or mishandling food -20%

- ↓ Thinking unkindly about others -18%

- ↓ Experiencing fear or anxiety -14%

A FAITH ENGAGED

Across surveys, we've found that among Christians, engaging Scripture most days of the week strongly predicts a more pro-active faith. Specifically, keeping in mind such factors as age, gender, church attendance, and prayer practices, the person engaged in the Bible has significantly higher odds of . . .

↑ Giving financially to a church +416%

↑ Memorizing Scripture +407%

↑ Discipling others +231%

↑ Sharing their faith with others +228%

↑ Giving financially to causes other than their church +218%

Our surveys of church congregations across the country reveal that most people frequently feel that they are not growing spiritually. In fact, at least once a year, nine out of ten regular church attenders feel like they are not growing spiritually. They spend an average of three to four months of the year spiritually "stuck."

Receiving, reflecting on, and responding to what God says in the Bible emerges again as the most powerful determinant of spiritual growth. Those who engage Scripture four or more days a week have significantly lower odds of . . .

↓ Feeling spiritually stagnant -60%

↓ Feeling like they can't please God -44%

A BIBLE-READING FAMINE

So how involved (or rather uninvolved) are Americans in reading or listening to the Bible? Figure 1 shows how often members of different age groups read or listen to the Bible in a given week. Clearly the majority of Americans do not hear from God at all through His Word. How many people do not read or listen to the Bible at all varies by age group, from slightly more than half of teens (ages thirteen to seventeen) to seven out of ten young adults (ages eighteen to twenty-four). A minority, ranging from one-fifth of adults to almost three-tenths of tweens (ages eight to twelve) and teens, engage Scripture one to three days a week. Relatively few read or listen to the Bible most days of the week.

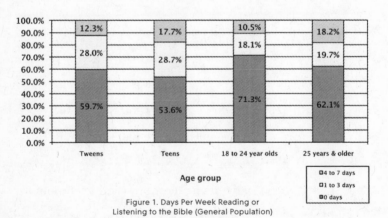

Figure 1. Days Per Week Reading or
Listening to the Bible (General Population)

As expected, scriptural engagement rates are higher among those who identify themselves as born-again Christians. However, considering that these are believers, the rates remain disturbingly low. In fact, most people who claim to follow Christ do not read or listen to the Bible most days of the week.

As shown in Figure 2, about one-fifth (teens) to two-fifths (young adults) of Christ-followers do not hear from God at all through His written Word in a given week. Three out of ten adults read or listen to the Bible one to three days a week. Tweens (40.1%) and teens (45.2%) are more likely to be engaged in Scripture at this level.

This leaves a minority of believers who do read or listen to the Bible at least four days a week. The size of this group ranges from one-quarter of tweens to about two-fifths of teens and adults who are twenty-five and older.

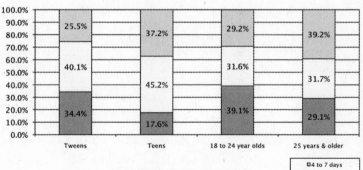

Figure 2. Days Per Week Reading or
Listening to the Bible
(Self-Identified Born-Again Christians)

4 to 7 days
1 to 3 days
0 days

NOTES